RetireSMART™!

How to Plan for a Tax-Free Retirement

Mark Anthony Grimaldi

Economist, No-load Fund Manager

First Edition

PAGE PUBLISHING, INC.
Conneaut Lake, PA

First originally published by Page Publishing 2019

ISBN 978-1-64334-900-8 (pbk)
ISBN 978-1-64462-891-1 (hc)
ISBN 978-1-64462-890-4 (digital)

Printed in the United States of America

This book is dedicated to my Wife,
my mom and all the amazing wonderful
supportive loving women in my life.

This book would not be possible without
the assistance of Mr. Frank J. Fabio, CPA
and Ms. Julie Schaeffer.

Introduction

I will show you how to save for retirement TAX FREE, grow your retirement account TAX FREE, withdraw your retirement income TAX FREE, and pass the balance to your loved ones TAX FREE!!! That's it. Interested? Keep reading.

How is this possible you ask? Actually, it's so simple. All you need to do is apply three basic tax laws the proper way. Are these laws "loopholes" only available to the rich? Nope. They are accessible to everyone and are hiding in plain sight. In fact, I bet you have used one, if not two, doing your most recent tax filing. The problem is, you didn't use them properly. Warren Buffet did. Jeff Bezos did, and now you will.

Buckle your seatbelt, because you are about to get off the 401(k) treadmill and merge on to the superhighway with The Smart 401(k).

Why is it Smart?

— Because it has no contribution limits.
— Because it has no investment choice limitations.
— Because it lets you touch your money when you need it most.
— Because it knows the tax difference between income and capital gains.
— Because it puts no age restriction on your money.
— Because it has no distribution minimums.
— Because it understands tax code.

In my first book, *The Money Compass*, the chapter about 401(k) plans got the most attention. My readers couldn't believe their 401(k) plans benefited no one but Uncle Sam. And that made me want to write a book dedicated to explaining one of the biggest financial misdirection in history: the 401(k) plan.

In this book, that's my mission, and I think I'm successful. But my discussion can't be all negative. In addition to telling you how *not* to invest, I have to tell you how *to* invest (least if I want this book to be useful).

It's something I've thought about a lot, as a practicing economist for more than thirty years. I feel it on a visceral level, almost every day, because I see people who have clearly done so poorly. When I walk into retail and food-service establishments, for example, I often see older folks working physically demanding jobs for near minimum wage. Some may be trying to stay busy; others may want to cover some fun extras in their life. But are many working those jobs because they need to, or because they didn't save wisely for retirement? Or is it something different entirely? I would like to suggest it was how they thought about retirement saving. Or more directly it's how they were programmed to think about saving for retirement. I think that we are all being told a huge lie about saving for retirement, more specifically 401(k)s.

Did the US Congress deceive the American public into thinking that a 401(k) plan would reduce their tax burden when in fact this book will prove beyond all doubt that a 401(k) plan is in fact designed for Uncle Sam's "financial" gain? I have always said that for fifty years the Congress has been passing laws designed to get the middle class to pay for the poor. That is why the rich get richer and the middle class is heading toward extinction. A 401(k) plan is the linchpin of that plan. So, I am asking you right now to clear your mind of all that you have been told about 401(k)s and continue reading as if you are learning about retirement savings for the first time. Because if you can *change your thinking*, you can *change your retirement. I guarantee it.*

My plan will work for every working American. However, the further you are from retirement, the bigger the impact it will have on your retirement. That is why this book is geared toward millennials and Gen X. My system is so simple that it can be broken down to three letters, G, P, S. Simple, right? In this book—or I think a better word is *guide*—I will simply lay out what each letter stands for and how to imply it to your financial life. *Spoiler alert!* By the end of this guide you will learn how the rich retire by earning interest, *not* paying interest, and why Warren Buffet famously claimed that his secretary pays a higher tax rate than he does. Are you ready? Shut off your phone, stop reading your e-mails, and open your mind. I am about to give you access to a financial world that the rich live in every day. I present to you: The Smart 401(k).

Chapter I

Why Am I a Loan?

Fixing America's Retirement Inequality

There's a problem brewing in America.

Today's younger generations—millennials and Generation X—see the problems their parents and grandparents are having making ends meet in retirement, and they don't have much faith that Social Security will be there for them when it's time for them to stop working.

So, they're searching for alternatives. You would think they would find myriad options, from 401(k) plans to annuities, but therein lies the rub—not everyone has access to such financial instruments.

Across the country, a large portion of working-age adults haven't saved nearly enough to retire, such that half of them risk being unable to maintain their preretirement standard of living once they stop working, according to the Center for Retirement Research at Boston College, and it's worse for those with lower incomes. The steady shift away from defined-benefit plans (such as pensions) to defined-contribution plans (such as 401(k) plans), along with rising inflation and stagnant earnings, is squeezing the families who need help most. The result: solid savings growth for the most affluent households (those with the top 20% of incomes), but flat retirement savings for everyone else, according to the Survey of Consumer Finances.

How did you get here, and where do you go from here, if you're not in the top 20%?

In the Beginning There Was Income Inequality

The story begins with income inequality, which is simply a way to say there is an extreme concentration of *income and wealth* in the hands of a small percentage of a population.

In the United States, median household income was $61,372 in 2017, according to the US Census Bureau. That represented an increase in real terms of 1.8% from the 2016 median of $60,309, and 2017 was the third consecutive year we saw an annual increase in median household income. So, things are good, right?

Not if you consider that income inequality has increased significantly since the 1970s after several decades of stability (although this trend diminishes significantly if in-kind compensation, as employer-paid health-care premiums, is factored in).

Americans who fall near the bottom of income distribution have seen their wages decline over the past few decades, according to the Urban Institute, while the share of earnings going to the top 0.1% boomed by than 400% between 1971 and 2001.

The most popular measure of inequality is called the Gini coefficient or index, which measures the extent to which the distribution of income or consumption expenditure, among individuals or households within an economy, deviates from a perfectly equal distribution.

That may sound technical, but it's fairly simple: A Gini rating of 0 means the society in question is perfectly equal, or everyone has exactly the same income. A Gini rating of 100 means the society in question is perfectly unequal, or one person takes home all of the income.

The United States has a Gini rating of 45, according to the CIA World Factbook. How does that compare to other countries? Well, Sweden has the lowest Gini coefficient of 27, and Lesotho, a landlocked country within South Africa, has the highest of 63.2.

It's important to understand what these numbers mean. Low income inequality isn't always better. For example, some African nations have high income equality rating because there aren't many rich people in those countries; everyone is poor. That's certainly not desirable. I'd prefer to live in a country where the rich are very rich and the poor are fairly comfortable.

That said, people do get concerned when it seems like an elite few have a lot of the pie, so to speak. So why is that the case in the United States? It's hard to say. The numbers even out a bit when we factor in in-kind compensation (such as employer-sponsored health-care premiums), but not as much as many would like. But for some reason, while incomes tend to rise over time, even after being adjusted for inflation, they rise more slowly for people near the bottom of the earnings scale.

Retirement Inequality Is Rising

Just as the income gap between the well-to-do and working people is growing, so too is retirement inequality—the portion of American workers who aren't prepared to retire versus those who are.

It's easy to see that lower earnings translate later to lower retirement incomes. Social Security benefits, along with other retirement savings balances, are generally tied to previous earnings, which, as we've shown, are increasingly imbalanced.

But retirement inequality and income inequality aren't necessarily correlated. Having a low income doesn't always mean you can't live comfortably. If you earned a low income but still lived within your means and saved, and you can rely on Social Security, you might be all right in retirement.

What matters is how much of your earnings you will be able to replace in retirement, with Social Security and/or savings. Even if you look at the situation this way, though, lower-income workers are behind, with 56% at risk of having a lower standard of living when they retire, according to the Center for Retirement Research at Boston College. The decline is slightly less for middle-income workers (54%) but fall sharply (to 41%) for high-income workers.

According to the Urban Institute, Americans aged sixty-seven to seventy-five, who are in the top fifth of the income distribution, will see their income *increase* by 3% in 2045, 5% in 2065, and 7% in 2085. But Americans aged sixty-seven to seventy-five, who are in in the bottom fifth of the income distribution, will see their income *decrease* by 3% in 2045, 6% in 2065, and 13% in 2085.

What's going on? Today, financial security in retirement increasingly depends, in great part, on how much people can save in their 401(k) plans during their working years. But it's harder for lower-income workers to save that way for a number of reasons:

- High-income workers save 6.11% of their wages in their retirement plans versus just 2.8% for low-income workers, likely because the less money you make, the higher percentage of your income you must devote to basics such as housing and health care.
- Lower-income workers experience significant drops in earnings five times over their careers. During those drops, they presumably contribute less to retirement savings, affecting what they can accumulate over time.
- Lower-income workers spend more time out of work than high-income works. During those pauses, as during earnings drops, these workers presumably contribute less to retirement savings.
- Lower-income workers' employers tend not to offer a retirement savings plan. Only 42% of lower-income older people are employed at any given time, making it difficult for them to save consistently, and when they are employed, only 44% work for employers offering such plans, according to the Center for Retirement Research.
- Retirement security may partially depend on delaying Social Security because the resulting larger monthly checks continue for as long as you're alive. But one study found that lower-income workers' life spans aren't increasing as rapidly higher-income workers' life spans. As a result, lower-income workers are less motivated to delay Social Security.

Whatever the cause, the problem exists, and it's worse for some generations than others. Did you think the baby boomers were in bad shape? Read on if you're younger.

Chapter II

The Google Generation

Generation by Generation

It's normal for people just starting out to have less money saved for retirement. But some research assesses inequality trends for specific generations, and the findings are interesting. Generation X looks better off than today's retirees; millennials don't.

Generation X was certainly behind in retirement savings when its members entered the workforce, especially given that they were very affected by the 2008 financial crisis, which hit many when were they starting to look for jobs and save. But members of Generation X have managed to make up most of the shortfall in subsequent years, thanks to their participation in the longest economic expansion we've seen in decades.

While a single study can't tell an entire story, one I find interesting is by Richard Johnson, an economist with the Urban Institute. He compared the incomes of today's retirees with income projections for the youngest members of Generation X, who will enter retirement in about thirty years. And the imbalance between those at the top and bottom is expected to be wider for Generation X than it is for today's retirees.

Generation X retirees in the top 10% of incomes will have future incomes that are 50% higher than the same cohort of today's retirees—$172,000 for Generation X versus $114,500 for today's retirees (in today's dollars).

But Generation X retirees in the lowest 25% of incomes will have future incomes just 24% percent higher than the same cohort incomes of today's retirees—$25,000 for Generation X versus $19,800 for today's retirees.

Meanwhile, millennials and the next generational cohort, Generation Z, are burdened by student debt and stagnant wages. They can only contribute the bare minimum to their retirement plans.

Even when taking their normal slow start into account, younger Americans are falling behind, according to the St. Louis Fed. The recent years of stock-market growth have barely helped millennials, and the St. Louis Fed says they're unlikely to make it up. According to the Fed, it's "a missed opportunity because asset appreciation is unlikely to be as rapid in the near future." (I keep telling my readers to not get used to a rising stock market because it always reverses. Now you've heard it from the Fed.)

Younger generations also have to deal with the fact that by the time they retire, Social Security could be different. Social Security is important to retirees. Today, the average monthly Social Security payment is $1,404, and more than 40% of single adults receive more than 90% of their income from that check, according to the Social Security Administration. There's no reason to think that will be different in the future. But the program's trustees have estimated that by 2034, Social Security won't be able to pay out full benefits. Any solution will likely require higher taxes and/or fewer benefits. And that will come out of the pockets of younger workers because baby boomers will be out of the workforce and comfortably into their retirements by then.

Where Now?

In 2018, the director of the Center for Retirement Research offered a solution for younger workers: work longer.

That point proved distressing to many and was later clarified to: "The vast majority of millennials will be fine if they work to age seventy."

When you take growing life spans into account, maybe that makes sense. In other words, seventy is the new sixty-five.

But *are* life spans expanding? Life expectancies recently took a turn for the worse, and there's a widening health gap between educated, affluent Americans and lower-income Americans. It could be a statistical anomaly, but if it isn't, what a triple whammy: the rich get richer, retire richer, *and* live longer.

There may not be a single answer, but in this book, I'll explore the options and provide a guide to getting on track for a comfortable retirement regardless of your income or savings.

Who Are Millennials?

To understand why, let's take a step back and look at how the millennial generation was raised and influenced.

Although generational definitions abound, according to Pew Research, millennials were born from 1981 to 1996, making them twenty-three to thirty-eight years old in 2019.

Sometimes called echo boomers because they're the offspring of the baby boomers, millennials are the largest demographic cohort in the United States, representing about 25% of the population.

Technology is a well-known factor in distinguishing millennials from other generations. Many have memories of landlines and perhaps even touch-tone and rotary phones; the oldest millennials were twenty-six when the iPhone was introduced in 2007. But they grew up with the Internet as a way of life, and they are early adaptors of new products, inside and outside of technology.

Where millennials aren't early adaptors is in finance. That's not because they don't know how to save. You might think of millennials as mindlessly spending their paychecks on expensive coffee and avocado toast, but up to 58% of them are also saving for retirement, according to Ramsey Solutions. But that doesn't mean they're saving enough, and it doesn't mean they're investing the right way.

To understand why, think about what millennials have experienced—the technology bubble bursting around the time they were in high school, and the Great Recession around the time they entered the workforce. Those are hard experiences to get over. Indeed, the Great Recession left an estimated 15% of millennials in their early twenties unemployed. Many are still struggling to get caught up today, and if history is any indication, their late start will likely hurt them long after they do find work. Studies of individuals who were unemployed during the early 1980s recession show that they were still financially behind twenty years later. Perhaps a result of these experiences, millennials don't trust financial institutions, including the Social Security Administration. Despite the fact that millennials are paying into Social Security now, 80% don't expect to get anything out of it, according to a study by the Transamerica Center for Retirement Studies. Those fears are justified. At current funding levels, Social Security will begin paying out more than it takes in around 2021, and benefits could be cut an estimated 23% around 2034. Something has to change.

Not surprisingly, millennials are also uncomfortable with investing risk, with a number of studies highlighting their desire to play it safe. According to Wells Fargo, more than half of millennials say that they will never be comfortable investing in the stock market, and according to Bankrate, around a quarter of millennials consider cash the best long-term investment.

Michael Dimock, president of the Pew Research Center, has said the recession's effect on millennials "will be a factor in American society for decades."

Who are Generation X?

Millennials can be best contrasted with Generation X, the demographic cohort that precedes them.

The start and end birth dates for Generation X vary from the early to mid-1960s to the early 1980s, but regardless, this generation is the smallest to date.

Generation X is sometimes referred to as the lost generation because it was the first to experience day care and divorce (remember the TV specials about latchkey kids?). In a 2014 report, Pew Research called them "America's neglected 'middle child.'"

This generational cohort is often characterized by high levels of skepticism and pragmatism (not to mention some of the worst hairstyles to ever gain popularity).

As they age, however, Generation X is making an impact. Although they're not the digital natives to the extent that millennials are, they're comfortable with technology, and Nielsen found that they're more likely to spend more time on every type of electronic device—phone, computer, or tablet—than millennials. The reason: they're using it to work. While Generation X is just as capable as millennials are with technology, they also show conventional leadership skills that are on par with those of the baby boomers.

Financially, however, Generation x is struggling just like millennials are: Total non-mortgage debt (which includes credit card and student loan debt) is high among this cohort, and 50% don't believe they can start saving for retirement until they pay off their credit card debt.

While saving and investing for retirement is important for millennials, it is less important than it is for other generations, according to a BMO Wealth Management Study. Among millennials, 47% cited retirement as a savings goal versus 66% of Generation X and 64% of baby boomers. Among millennials, shorter-term goals, such as saving for a vacation (21%) or a new/upgraded home (26%) were also reasons to save and invest.

Response no. 1

Beth: How I would describe what a 401(k) is...

From my perspective, a 401(k) is one method of saving toward retirement. The mechanics of it require you to allocate a certain percentage of your paycheck (that is then not taxed) to be put into an account managed by a financial services company with your money being allocated to various stocks, bonds, and/or mutual funds. The hope is that this account not only increases in value due to putting money in every paycheck but also by investing in companies that are likely to see stable growth. The end goal, of course, is to have a good pool of funds saved up in the account for when you reach retirement. As far as I understand, if you withdraw money from your 401(k) before retirement, you have to pay a penalty to account for the taxes that you did not originally pay on that income.

Beth: If I have a 401(k) and why...

I do have a 401(k). To be honest, I have one because it seems like something everyone else has, and my employer automatically sets up your 401(k) when you join the company. Having said that, I probably contribute less to my 401(k) than is typically encouraged for a variety of reasons: (1) as my employer does not have a 401(k) match, I see less incentive to max out the 401(k); (2) as someone without parental financial support, I would rather focus on putting money into a savings account that can be easily accessed when I decide to put a down payment on property, something which I hope to do in the next few years; (3) I have become weary of 401(k)s after watching this segment of a TV show and have ensured my funds are not in accounts that have high broker fees; (4) I don't trust the stock market and struggle to not consider it gambling, which is something I'm strongly morally opposed to. I think it's good to have a variety of retirement options, including a 401(k), property, savings accounts, and other options so that I haven't put all of my eggs into one basket.

Response no. 2

Oliver: How I would describe what a 401(k) is...

I would describe a 401(k) as a savings account designed to put money aside for retirement with taxes to incentivize keeping the funds in the account until one is of retirement age. They are typically set up as automatic withdrawals of a percentage of an individual's paycheck.

Oliver: If I have a 401(k) and why...

I do have a 401(k), primarily because it is the most accessible way for me to save for retirement from the options provided to me from my company. Since my company does not do 401(k) matching and instead contributes to an ESOP, I see both accounts as saving for retirement. However, I see the 401(k) as more stable and reliable, as the ESOP fluctuates based on the health of the company on an annual basis.

Response no. 3

Josephine: How I would describe what a 401(k) is...

It is a pension/retirement plan.

Josephine: If I have a 401(k) and why...

I do not have a 401(k), I have a 403(b), which is the nonprofit version of a 401(k). I have one because it is offered by my company, and it seems like I should put money in it. Also, my company contributes 5% automatically as a staff benefit. It is a Roth account, which means that I pay taxes now rather than when I withdraw the money later on because I want the government to get my taxes now rather than in the future

Chapter III

The Whys have it

A Common Challenge: Not Enough Savings

Not saving enough is a common pitfall across Generation X, and millennials are no exception. But the savings problem is likely enhanced when it comes to both.

That's because they will likely live longer than previous generations, and thus will need to save more. We may think of millennials as younger, but they are actually the first generation in history that will likely reach age ninety in large numbers, and could spend a third of their lives as older people.

And they're not prepared. We will have an estimated eight million people in their nineties by the year 2050, and Social Security and Medicare aren't prepared to handle those numbers. As a result, millennials have to take responsibility for preparing themselves.

Are they ready? Not really. There is some good news: According to Fidelity, as of the second quarter of 2018, millennials (defined for these purposes as those ages twenty-one to thirty-seven) with 401(k) plans were contributing 7.3% of their paychecks to those plans and had an average balance of $25,500. With employers matching, on average, 4.1%, the savings rate for millennials with 401(k)s was 11.3%. That's not bad, but remember, this only counts millennials who are saving in the first place. According to the aforementioned Ramsey Solutions study, 42% of them aren't saving at all, and that number is even higher (around 66%) in other studies.

A Unique Mistake

In avoiding risk in the form of equities, millenials are making the same mistake many people who experience market downturns make. Just think of the ultraconservative silent generation, born between 1935 and 1945, many of whom experienced the Great Depression and were known to hide money under mattresses. The fear of market volatility is strong.

Despite the market crashes of 2000 and 2008, and others before them, equities are still a good investment. Yes, the markets fell sharply in 2000 and 2008, but they then recovered. Over time, equities are one of the best ways to ensure your money grows over time. The S&P 500 Index has returned 235% since March of 2009, an annualized 15% with dividends reinvested. And the average annualized return for the S&P 500 Index over the past ninety years has been roughly 9.8%.

They tend to ignore this fact from investment history and draw too much on their own bad experiences of the markets when planning for retirement.

So, the first advice to give millennials when helping them plan for retirement is invest. Cash can be tempting for the stability it offers, but if you are saving for the long term (such as retirement), a diversified portfolio of stocks is your best shot at a decent return to help your savings grow and provide a secure nest egg.

Financial Planning for Millennials and Gen X

Everything I discuss in this book applies to millennials. For example, investing in a 401(k) plan beyond what you receive in a company match is not ideal. But this generational cohort needs some extra advice. Here are several tips.

Know How Much You'll Need to Retire

Most millennials (84%) have saved less than $50,000 for retirement, according to MetLife. And only 20% believe they'll need to save $500,000 or more for a comfortable retirement (with a third believing they can retire comfortably on $200,000 or less). This is a fairy tale. If you're thirty-five and plan to retire in thirty-two years at age sixty-seven, you'll need around $2.2 million for 75% income replacement at retirement. To provide that nest egg, assuming 3% annual inflation, 2% annual salary increases, and a 5% rate of return, you will need to save 25% of your yearly income (less any employer match, if applicable), or around $1,600 a month. Of course, that savings rate will change based on the inputs—inflation rate, salary increase, and rate of return—but this illustrates that you'll need much more than $200,000 to retire comfortably.

And it's very simple! First off, here are the items you must know before I lay out the three simple steps, each of which will comprise a chapter in this book.

Why You Need to Pay Off Your Debt

Debt. Almost everyone has it, but no one wants to talk about it, so I start by addressing it head-on.

Why do I start with debt?

Debt is America's dirty secret. That's partly because growth in the cost of living has outpaced income growth. But it's also because there's been a change in the way we think about debt. When I was growing up, people bought cars for cash, and sometimes houses too. Today, debt is normal, and you can even get a thirty-five-year mortgage. That's causing us to live beyond our means.

But the day of reckoning ultimately comes—the day we stop bringing money in and only send money out. And that day is called retirement. Because they've taken on debt, most people spend their retirement before it even begins. That makes debt the single biggest problem that stands between you and your financial freedom. In fact, when people ask me to tell them when they can retire, I ask them to tell me the date they will be debt free.

But what is debt? And isn't some debt better than other debt?

When I talk about debt, I refer to consumer debt, which includes mortgages, auto loans, student loans, and credit cards. A mortgage is one of the best kinds of debt, as I'll explain. I'll also explain why other debt is generally bad. And I'll provide some easy-to-follow steps to getting debt free.

Why You Need to Understand Taxation

Once you have money (by not spending it on debt), you need to understand how to keep as much of it in your pocket as possible. And to do that, you need to avoid paying unnecessary taxes.

When it comes to taxation, you really need to understand how just two things will affect your retirement (which is good, because today's tax code is 74,608 pages long; this limits it).

Ordinary income is taxed at different rates depending on the amount of income you earn in a given tax year and how you file (single, married, etc.). You may have been told you should reduce ordinary income with a 401(k) plan, but that's a fool's errand. No matter how you invest, all the money in your 401(k) plan will eventually be taxed as income—and other than the federal estate tax, the income tax is the highest you can pay.

You're better off investing your money outside of a 401(k) plan and paying capital gains taxes, which are lower than ordinary income taxes. In this chapter, I'll explain, in great detail, why.

Why You Need to Get the Government Out of Your Retirement Plan

Because older Americans are facing a financial crisis—in part because they've taken on too much debt, in part because they haven't saved enough—the government is getting involved in your retirement.

A number of states are now forcing small businesses to create retirement plans for private sector employees, and under the fiduciary rule, financial advisors who work with retirement plans are subject to a much higher level of accountability.

These may sound like good things, but they have significant negative implications. For example, the fiduciary rule may push investors into making one of two bad choices: receiving no professional advice or using fee-based accounts. And that could be costly. If your financial advisor charges an annual management of 1%, which is fairly average, and you have $500,000 in retirement savings, you would pay $5,000 in fees every year.

I'll explain those negative implications in more detail, which, I hope, will lead you to the same conclusion I've reached: that investors should steer their retirement savings away from any and all government involvement. Every time the government gets involved in your retirement, it will cost you—either in more fees or more taxes or both.

Why You Need to Understand the Evolution of the 401(k) Plan

I'll also spend a lot of time talking about 401(k) plans, because they're the foundation of many Americans' retirement savings, and are very misunderstood.

I'll start by explaining the basics, including the history of 401(k) plans, which involves some key turning points, such as the Pension Protection Act of 2006. It allowed employers to automatically enroll employees in 401(k) plans. You may think that's a good thing; in this book, you'll find out why it's not.

Of course, I'll discuss the benefits of 401(k) plans—primarily, tax deferral—but I'll spend more time talking about the problems. Some may be obvious: required minimum distributions (RMDs), fees, and effectiveness.

Effectiveness? Yes. Even Ted Benna, the so-called father of the 401(k), is no longer an unabashed fan. Although he believes the retirement-savings vehicles are benefiting millions of employees, he's concerned that they've become too complicated. "We said, we are going to make people smart and savvy enough to make the right investment decisions, but it just hasn't worked," he is quoted as saying.

Why You Need to Stop Contributing to Your 401(k) Plan

Once I've explained why 401(k) plans are so attractive, and thrown out a few criticisms, I'll get to the heart of the matter: you should stop contributing to your 401(k) plan immediately.

You heard me right. Investing in your 401(k) plan is a mistake that could cost you hundreds of thousands of dollars in taxes.

That may sound counterintuitive. You've been taught to save money for retirement via a 401(k) plan. You get a tax deduction today, and the money grows tax deferred. Then, when you withdraw the money in retirement, you'll likely be in a lower tax bracket. In the end, then, you reduce how much you pay in taxes.

The problem with the traditional logic is that it doesn't tell you how things will work out in the end. As I explain, it's like Evel Knievel telling you how easy it is to jump a motorcycle over fifty buses. The jumping is easy; it's the landing that can be very painful. Similarly, when it comes to 401(k) plans, people generally talk about only the accumulation phase (the jump); no one is willing to talk about the distribution phase (the landing).

I'll discuss both the jump and the landing, proving that a 401(k) plan will generate more tax revenue for the IRS than an investment in an after-tax account.

Why You Need to Stop Putting Small-Business Profits in Retirement Plans

While the main theme of this book is to expose the lies you've been told about 401(k) plans, my work would be incomplete if I didn't address the lies you've been told about retirement plans for small businesses.

If you're a small business owner, you don't have the luxury of an employer-sponsored retirement plan to help ensure your financial future, and a traditional 401(k) plan is likely out of your reach given the administrative hassles associated with creating and maintaining one.

But you do have some options, including the SIMPLE 401(k), the Self-Employed 401(k), the SIMPLE IRA, and the SEP IRA.

Qualified retirement plans such as these benefit employees and employers alike.

But I'll ask an important question: Instead of putting money in retirement plans like these, might you be better off keeping it and using a new tax deduction made available with the Tax Cuts and Jobs Act of 2017, which went into effect in January 2018?

The new law allows pass-through entities to take a deduction of 20% against their business income. This essentially reduces the effective top rate on pass-through entities' income by roughly 10 percentage points over pre-2018 tax law.

I'll show you how hypothetical business owners who each have a profit at the end of the year would fare using both approaches—putting the profit in a SEP IRA or taking the money as income and receiving a Schedule K-1 from the IRS.

Why You Need to Avoid Target-Date Retirement Funds

Now that you know to avoid a 401(k) plan, you may ask where you should invest. And you might be tempted to turn to target-date funds, which automatically rebalance their holdings to become more conservative as an investor gets closer to retirement.

These are perhaps the lowest-maintenance retirement-saving product you can purchase, and that makes them very popular. You can set it and forget it, so to speak.

But it's all a lie. "Set it and forget it" doesn't work.

Don't believe me? In 2008, two of the largest well-known target-date funds available, which had target dates of 2010, both lost more than 20%, thanks to the equity-market crash. But why hadn't a retirement fund with a target date of 2010 reduced its exposure to equities two years before the target date—especially if stocks were near all-time highs?

So, I'll go into detail about why target-date retirement funds are gimmicks whose popularity far overshoots their effectiveness. In fact, I'll expose them as ticking time bombs (with misleading fees) that are actually acting counter to their intended purpose by adding risk as time goes by. And I'll explain what's behind it: the greed of companies that manage target-date funds.

Why You Need to Take These Three Steps to a Secure Low-Tax Retirement

Now that you've learned why a 401(k) will cause you great dismay, and target-date funds are a terrible way to save for retirement, you may be asking, "Where *do* I invest my nest egg?"

I'll finish this book by showing you—in three easy steps—how to create a secure retirement that is taxed at the lowest possible federal rate, eliminating the cancer that eats away at your nest egg in your golden years.

Each step is simple, and anyone can take it. First, grow your portfolio after taxes. Second, pay off debt. And third, save your age divided by three.

It may sound simple. I've already told you how to avoid paying unnecessary taxes on your retirement savings and how to pay off your debt. But the third step isn't as easy at is sounds because of something I call the procrastination penalty. That makes saving your age divided by three more and more difficult the longer you wait to start saving.

If you follow these steps, however, you'll be ahead of most other Americans—and ready to retire when the time comes.

Chapter IV

What's Roth with You?

What's a Roth 401(k)—and Why You Might (or Might Not) Want One

A Roth 401(k) is an employer-sponsored retirement-savings account that—unlike a traditional 401(k)—is funded with after-tax dollars. That might make you ask: Why would you ever want something like that? Isn't the whole point of retirement saving to use tax-advantaged accounts? Hopefully, I can answer that question and many more because if you want to make the most of your retirement savings, you should understand the difference between these two types of accounts. Ready? Read on.

From IRAs to 401(k)s

Traditional and Roth 401(k) plans work much like traditional and Roth individual retirement accounts (IRAs): they differ in when and how and when you get a tax break.

With a traditional IRA, you invest before you pay taxes on your money. In other words, your contributions are tax deductible in the year they are made. However, your withdrawals in retirement are taxed.

With a Roth IRA, you invest after you pay taxes on your money. Your contributions are not tax deductible in the year they are made, but your withdrawals in retirement are not taxed.

As you might extrapolate, Roth IRAs are generally thought to be well-suited to people who think they will be in a higher tax bracket in retirement than they are now.

Moving to 401(k)s

You know what a traditional 401(k) is: It's an employer-sponsored retirement-savings plan; so your contributions are taken out of your paycheck before you get it. That helps many people save because when you don't see the money, you can't spend it.

A traditional 401(k) has a contribution limit. In 2019, the maximum you can contribute is $19,000 per year or $25,000 if you're over age fifty.

And you often get a company match—meaning, your company contributes a percentage of what you contribute. Around 80% of companies that offer a 401(k) or similar plan offer some sort of a match on employee contributions. That's free money, and if you've read the other things I've written about 401(k) plans, it's the primary reason to invest in one.

With 401(k) plans, employees can invest in stocks, bonds, or a combination of stocks and bonds, depending on the level of risk you can tolerate.

Finally, when you withdraw money from a traditional 401(k), you'll have to pay taxes on the amount you withdraw based on your tax rate in retirement. That's also appealing to many people because they expect to be in a lower tax bracket in retirement than they are when working.

Another benefit of 401(k) plans is that they offer some flexibility if you're in a financial pinch. You have two options. First, you can take a loan from your 401(k) plan, if permitted by the plan (and 87% of 401(k) plans offer loan options, according to the Employee Benefit Research Institute, or EBRI). Second, IRS rules allow you to take what's called a "hardship withdrawal" from your 401(k) plan (though your employer has to allow it as well).

With such features, 401(k) plans are extremely popular. Many financial pundits—financial advisors, corporate human resources managers, and financial institutions tout their advantages as a great way to save for retirement.

The Roth 401(k)—that was introduced in 2006 with the goal of combining the features of a traditional 401(k) and a Roth IRA—is similar in many ways. Your contributions are taken out of your paycheck, and the contribution limit is the same as with a traditional 401(k). And you may get a company match, if your employer offers one.

But that's where the similarities end. Let's look more closely at the differences between these two retirement-savings options.

Taxation

The biggest difference between a traditional 401(k) and a Roth 401(k) is taxation, just as it is with a traditional IRA and traditional 401(k).

Like a Roth IRA, a Roth 401(k) is an after-tax retirement savings account. Your contributions are taxed before they are deposited in your Roth 401(k) account. Because you're paying taxes now, when you contribute to a Roth 401(k), you're taking home a little less in your paycheck.

That may not sound appealing, but wait a minute, the greatest benefit of a Roth 401(k) isn't what happens now but what happens when you start withdrawing money in retirement.

Withdrawals

Because you already paid taxes on your contributions, *the withdrawals you make in retirement are tax-free*. Well, somewhat. The money *you* contributed will be tax-free; the money *your employer* contributed and any earnings will still be taxed.

Let's use an example to illustrate. Say you have $1 million saved at retirement—good job! If that $1 million is invested in a traditional 401(k), you'll pay taxes on your withdrawals in retirement. If you're in the 22% tax bracket, $230,000 of that $1 million would go to pay taxes. Now if you have that $1 million invested in a Roth 401(k) instead, the $1 million is yours to keep.

Once caveat: It might be easier to get to that $1 million in a traditional IRA because you might invest more to start with. Look at it this way. If you're okay with $100 being taken out of your paycheck to go to a traditional 401(k), it will be taken out before you pay taxes on it, so the entire $100 will be deposited into your account to grow. But if $100 is taken out of your paycheck and invested in a Roth 401(k), it's not really $100 you're starting with—it's $100 minus your tax rate. So, you're starting your growth from a lower level.

Access

There's one more difference between a traditional 401(k) and a Roth 401(k) that should be mentioned—access to your money. With a traditional 401(k), you can't start receiving distributions until you reach age 59 1/2 unless you want to pay a penalty. *The same is true with a Roth 401(k), but you also must have held the account for five years.* If retirement is a long way in the future, that may not matter. But if you're approaching retirement and thinking of contributing to a Roth 401(k), now you may want to remember that you won't have access to the money for five more years.

Why Choose a Roth 401(k)?

I've made it pretty clear that I'm not a fan of 401(k) plans. I won't rehash the reasons here. But if you're going to invest in one, there are a few reasons you might prefer a Roth 401(k) over a traditional 401(k).

The primary reason is the taxation and withdrawal difference. No one knows how tax brackets will change in the future, especially if you're still decades away from retirement. So why not get the taxation out of the way now so you know what you're working with?

And it's never fun to see your money grow, then have to see a big chunk of it taken away in taxes, as happens with the traditional 401(k) at retirement.

Now for the Bad News

Now, before you go out and invest in your employer's Roth 401(k), you may want to heed a second piece of advice, which may seem like financial heresy: Don't contribute to a 401(k) at all, whether it's a traditional or Roth 401(k)!

The reason isn't the same one that led me to tell you not to invest in a traditional 401(k). In that case, my concern is that a traditional 401(k) doesn't tell you how things will work out in the end. When it comes to 401(k) plans, people generally only talk about the accumulation phase; no one is willing to talk about the distribution phase. But both the jump and the landing are important, and when you consider both of them, you see that a traditional 401(k) plan will generate more tax revenue for the IRS than an investment in a properly tax-managed account.

Now a Roth 401(k) isn't exactly the same because you invest after-tax dollars. But it has problems of its own—namely, a mountain of IRS regulations that make it difficult to set up (if you're an employer) and a mountain of fees that cut into your returns (if you're an investor).

As for regulations, consider how difficult it is to even find the IRS rules that govern retirement plans. I think it's somewhere here:

> US Code
> Title 26. INTERNAL REVENUE CODE
> Subtitle A. Income Taxes
> Chapter 1. NORMAL TAXES AND SURTAXES
> Subchapter D. Deferred Compensation, Etc.
> Part I. PENSION, PROFIT-SHARING,
> STOCK BONUS PLANS, ETC.
> Subpart A. General Rule
> Section 401. Qualified pension, profit-sharing,
> and stock bonus plans

That last section alone is roughly eighteen thousand words, by my count—a short novel. Now imagine reading that in order to figure out how 401(k) plans—traditional or Roth—work.

As for fees, 401(k) plans offer mutual funds, many of them that come with high fees. That's because they invest in "load" mutual funds. A load fund comes with a sales charge or commission. The fund investor pays the load, which goes to compensate a sales intermediary, such as a broker, financial planner, or investment advisor.

Think about it. The mutual fund has to make money. So if you're an asset manager having $5 trillion in assets under management (I won't name any names) and charge just 0.10% to manage that money, your yearly revenues would be $5 billion. But most asset managers charge fees that are six or seven times that on their mutual funds—the mutual funds that are in your 401(k) plan.

You can sometimes get lower-cost investments in your 401(k) plan—index or exchange-traded funds—there generally aren't a lot of choices. And most investors don't know that's an option. If I asked a sample of 401(k) plan participants to name the names of their 401(k) funds and the investment fees each one incurs, I doubt many of them could do it.

So, though the Roth 401(k) is an improvement over a traditional 401(k), it's not ideal. Investing in your 401(k) plan is a mistake that could cost you and your loved ones hundreds of thousands of dollars in taxes.

Plus, Roth 401(k) plans are also subject to another concern of mine—automatic enrollment.

People just aren't contributing to their 401(k) plans. Just 45% of workers offered a 401(k) say they contribute money, according to the EBRI's 2016 Retirement Confidence Survey. As a result, many employers automatically enroll employees in their 401(k) plans. According to Aon's 2015 Trends & Experience in DC Plans Survey, 52% of employers automatically enroll workers at a savings rate of 4% or more, up from 39% of employers in 2013.

So when it comes to Roth 401(k) plans, I suggest you heed my general advice about 401(k) plans: Invest only up to the amount that you receive in an employer match. If you have more to invest, invest it elsewhere.

Chapter V

The Road Less Traveled

Ready?

Are you still with me? I hope so, because this will be a fun ride. You'll learn some things that sound scandalous (stop contributing to your 401(k) plan?) and some steps to get you where you need to go (save your age divided by three). So let's get started.

Are you on the right road to retirement?

As the question implies, my guess is you think there is only one road to a successful retirement. Oh, how the rich have played all of us.

I'm here to tell you that there are two roads to a successful retirement. About 99% of us travel one road while the rich travel the other (that is much less bumpy). But let me let tell you a secret: the other road is open for all of us to use, if we can just find it.

How do you find it, you ask? In this guide, I'm going to show you a road map I call the "Expressway to Retirement." But before I do that, let's look at the alternative—the road that 99% of us use.

I call it the 401(k) road. This road is long—very long. In fact, most Americans take thirty to forty years to travel it. It's filled with thousands of toll booths (fees) and very few exits (withdrawals). So as you travel along it, the tolls keep adding up, mile after mile. And if you ever need to exit, look out! The exit tolls (income and excise taxes) are very expensive.

This road also bypasses many of the great destinations along the way to retirement. If you want to stop along the way and get off a "vacation exit," it will cost you an exit tax and penalty. If you need to pull over at the "need a new refrigerator" rest stop, get ready to cough up more in taxes and penalties.

You see, the 401(k) road is designed to keep you stuck in traffic because the longer you're on it, the bigger the pay day is for Uncle Sam when you exit.

Even worse, due to government regulations, the types of investment vehicles that are allowed on your 401(k) highway are extremely limited. It only allows a handful of vehicles (investments). Maybe you can choose from a minivan, a midsize SUV, or pickup truck, but you can't choose a Tesla, a European sports car, or a slow and steady smart car. If you want those, you're out of luck.

And even among the options that are available to you, most travelers have no idea what vehicle to choose, so the powers that be just stick you on a bus with thousands of other folks they feel is right for you. (I call these buses target-date retirement funds and will share more about these later).

In summary, the 401(k) highway is an overcrowded, one-lane road that is filled with potholes, toll booths, state troopers, unsafe turns, no guard rails, no rest stops, and very few exits. No wonder this country is having a retirement crisis. Its road to retirement is a highway to poverty and disappointment. It truly is a road to nowhere.

The rich's expressway to retirement, meanwhile, is quite the opposite. It's a wonderful road—well maintained, with no toll booths, exits in every town, and (best of all) no minimum or maximum speed limits.

It's not a new road. In fact, it's the oldest road known to man. It's been around as long as people have been saving for retirement. However, the road is getting less and less use every single day. Why? Uncle Sam and Wall Street don't want you to know it even exists.

Want proof? Ask the IRS the maximum amount of money you can put away for retirement. The bureaucrats will most likely give you the 401(k) rules because they want you on that road. The actual answer is, *as much as you want*! There is no limit to how much you can save for retirement—or anything else, for that matter. But there are very strict limits one you get on the 401(k) road.

If you drove down the rich's expressway to retirement today, you would only see the rich using it. And they don't want you on it. They want it all for themselves. To scare you away, they may deny its existence. They're so determined to keep you off their road. They'll tell you they built you your own road to retirement. It's called the 401(k) road. But why would you fall for that?

With that said, I don't want to leave you to your own devices. No offense, but how many people can manage their monthly budget properly let alone their retirement nest egg? I also don't want to leave you to the wolves of Wall Street. So I'm going to use my more than thirty years of experience and lay out a GPS for choosing a financial advisor who is right for you.

My advice to you is to ask someone in your life who seems financially secure who they use. Trust me when I say this person will be flattered that you came to him or her for advice. And you'll probably get a good referral. Successful people network with each other, so the odds are the person you go to (assuming he or she is as financially secure as you believe) will have the name of a financial advisor to share.

This approach is rooted in something my dad used to say when I was growing up. "Kids, let me give you some advice. Never take advice from someone less successful than you."

I don't know if he coined that expression or borrowed it from someone else, but it's dripping with wisdom.

Once you have the name of a financial advisor (or a few), your work isn't over. You'll still need to do some due diligence, and I'm going to explain how. Before we start, however, let me clarify what I mean by "financial advisor."

In contrast to stock brokers (who help you trade stocks), insurance agents (who help you buy life insurance and annuities), and accountants (who prepare your taxes), financial planners often advise their clients on how to save and invest their money. Whether you want help with a specific financial goal or need a broad analysis of your investments, a financial planner can help. Some even specialize in certain areas, such as retirement planning and estate planning.

Got it? Great. Here's how to find one.

Callout: Tip no. 1: Consider the advisor's pay structure. An advisor who earns money based on commission could have an incentive to steer you in a particular direction.

Step 1. Choose a Type of Financial Advisor

Anyone can hang out a shingle as a financial planner, but you can break financial advisors down into three groups based on how they are paid: commission-based advisors, fee-only advisors, and fee-based advisors.

Commission-Based Advisors

Commission-based advisors sell financial products—mutual funds, annuities, and insurance, for example—and receive commissions on those products.

They are sometimes referred to as "registered representatives" because they have their Series 6 or Series 7 license from the Financial Industry Regulatory Authority (FINRA), and they are often employed by large financial institutions.

Because some or all of a commission-based advisor's income is determined by what he or she sells you, many people consider them to have a conflict of interest. Do they want to sell you a mutual fund because it's what's best for you, or because it offers them the highest commission?

Fee-Only Advisors

Fee-only advisors make money not through commissions but through flat fees—sometimes hourly rates, sometimes a percentage of the assets they manage. For example, you might pay $1,500 for a financial plan, or you might pay 1% of all the assets—investment and other accounts—they're managing for you. Often, fee-only advisors provide more comprehensive advice than commission-based advisors do, including asset allocation, retirement planning, and estate planning, to name just a few areas.

Fee-Based Advisors

Fee-based advisors can be considered a hybrid of commission-based advisors and fee-only advisors. Like commission-based advisors, they are usually affiliated with a stock broker or insurance agent and receive a commission for selling financial products. But like the fee-only advisors, fee-based advisors also provide financial planning for a fee. So, as you would with commission-based advisors, you may want to be cautious of conflicts of interest.

Callout: Tip no. 2: Look for a financial adviser who is a Certified Financial Planner, or CFP for short.

Step 2. Determine What Your Advisor Will Do

Whether you want help with a specific financial goal (such as preparing to buy a house) or need a broad analysis of your investments, a financial planner can help. Some specialize in estate planning; others consult on a comprehensive array of financial issues. But essentially, you can look at their services in three ways.

You will want a *consultation* from an advisor who charges an hourly fee if you have specific questions about a specific financial problem, such as buying a house, going back to school, or selling a business.

If you need an advisor to create a one-time road map that will help you reach your financial goals—from insurance to investments—you're looking for *comprehensive financial planning*.

Finally, if you're looking for asset management—someone to allocate your portfolio and keep it balanced over time—you will want a *long-term financial partner*. He or she will invest and manage your money, providing continuous updates as your circumstances change as well as comprehensive reporting.

Locate Some Options

Next, you'll want to obtain a short list of advisors. One place to find an advisor is through the National Association of Personal Financial Advisors (www.napfa.org), a nationwide organization of fee-only advisors. You can also look on the CFP website (home of Certified Financial Planners—more on that later). Or you can ask for referrals from your accountant, attorney, colleagues, or friends.

CALLOUT: Tip no. 3: Read the code of ethics your financial advisor adheres to and look for the word "fiduciary." That means the advisor is required to look after your best interests.

Step 3. Review the Candidates' Credentials

Once you have a short list, you'll want to review credentials. Anyone can call himself or herself a financial advisor and may tack on combination of letters after their names. How do you make sense of it?

CFP, short for Certified Financial Planner, is a significant credential. Advisors must have several years of experience, pass a six-hour exam administered by the Certified Financial Planner Board of Standards about the specifics of personal finance, and complete continuing education. They are also held to strict *ethical standards*.

Even with a CFP designation, you'll want to look at experience. How long has the advisor been in practice? What was their previous experience? Education is important, as is practice.

Finally, consider fit. Advisors have different styles and philosophies. Does the advisor's style mesh with yours? Most advisors will provide a free initial consultation to tell you about their practice. After that conversation, do you like and trust your advisor? It's a close (and in many cases, long-term) relationship, and your financial advisor will know many personal details of your life.

Step 4. Meet the Advisor Face-to-Face

Meeting with your advisor face-to-face is important, but I realize in today's world, it's not always possible. But even if you can't meet in person, don't hire a financial advisor based on a slick website or several e-mails. Try to engage in a meaningful dialogue.

A good financial advisor will do more listening than talking. He or she will not offer you any solutions before getting to know you and your financial objectives.

Although the Securities and Exchange Commission (SEC) doesn't allow financial advisors to advertise via client testimonials, it is certainly fine to ask the advisor for three references. In fact, I'd ask for several: one from a long-term client of ten years or longer, one from a short-term client of less than one year, and one from a client that is similar to you in his or her objectives and time horizon.

Finally, ask the financial advisor the most important question there is: What is their track record? This is a tricky question because the SEC has strict rules about what a financial advisor can claim as a track record. But he or she should be able to provide you with something.

If a financial advisor chosen based on the steps above can readily provide you with three references and a track record, and you get a good feeling about the person, you may have found your trusted partner.

Chapter VI

As Easy as...1,2,3

Retirement GPS: Three Steps to a Secure Tax-Free Retirement

The tax system is rigged, but you can beat it. How? In this chapter, I will show you—in three easy steps—how to create a secure retirement that is taxed at the lowest possible federal rate, eliminating the cancer that eats away at your nest egg in your golden years. Each step is simple, and anyone can take it. But the sooner you attack the problem, the better the outcome.

Three Steps to a Secure Low-Tax Retirement

Step 1: **G**row your portfolio after taxes.
Step 2: **P**ay off debt.
Step 3: **S**ave your age divided by three.

Step 1: Grow Your Portfolio after Taxes

It's this simple: start saving today with after-tax money. After-tax money is your paycheck, and you should put a portion of it in a brokerage account.

How? Just contact any one of the large investment companies—Vanguard, Schwab, or Fidelity—and ask to open a regular brokerage account in your name. Most companies don't charge a fee to open or maintain this type of account.

Then ask to set up an automatic investment program in which you will invest a certain amount each month. How much depends on your individual financial circumstances.

As to *where* to invest the money, I suggest to use the lowest-cost S&P 500 Index fund or exchange-traded fund (ETF). Most of these types of funds have low minimum investments and even lower monthly contribution levels.

Making small investments at regular intervals over time—called dollar-cost averaging—can be an effective investment strategy. It establishes discipline, and by helping you to invest regularly, it can alleviate any worries trying to time the market.

It can even help you take advantage of market fluctuations. Because you invest the same dollar amount each period, you typically purchase more shares when prices are low and fewer shares when prices are high. This means that over the entire purchase period, your average cost per share could be lower than the investment's average price per share. Paying less than the average share price is desirable because it allows you to purchase more shares over time.

What does that mean? First, let's define the terms I just used.

- Your *average cost per share* is the amount you invested divided by the number of shares you received. So, if you invest $5,000 over five purchases, and receive a total of 788 shares, your average cost per share is $5,000 divided by 788, or $6.35.
- The *average share price* is the total price of the shares you bought divided by the number of purchases you made. So, if you make five purchases—at $5 a share, $6 a share, $7 a share, $8 a share, then $9 a share—your total share price is the sum of these numbers, or $33. The average share price is this $33 divided by the total number of purchases, or 5—so $6.60.

Now that you know the terms, it may be helpful to look at a few hypothetical examples to illustrate how dollar-cost averaging works. Let's say that you've decided to invest $5,000 in an equity mutual fund by making $1,000 investments per quarter over a five-quarter (15-month) period. How will three typical market environments—rising market, declining market, and volatile market—affect your investment?

Rising Market

Investment	Amount	Share Price	Shares Acquired
First quarter	$1,000	$5	200
Second quarter	$1,000	$6	167
Third quarter	$1,000	$7	143
Fourth quarter	$1,000	$6	167
Fifth quarter	$1,000	$9	111
Total	$5,000	$33	788

Average share cost to you ($5,000/788 shares): $6.35
Average share price ($33/5 purchases): $6.60

Declining Market

Investment	Amount	Share Price	Shares Acquired
First quarter	$1,000	$5	200
Second quarter	$1,000	$3	333
Third quarter	$1,000	$3	333
Fourth quarter	$1,000	$2	500
Fifth quarter	$1,000	$1	1,000
Total	$5,000	$14	2,366

Average share cost to you ($5,000/2,366 shares): $2.11
Average share price ($14/5 purchases): $2.80

Volatile Market

Investment	Amount	Share Price	Shares Acquired
First quarter	$1,000	$5	200
Second quarter	$1,000	$7	143
Third quarter	$1,000	$5	200
Fourth quarter	$1,000	$3	333
Fifth quarter	$1,000	$5	200
Total	$5,000	$25	1,076

Average share cost to you ($5,000/1,076 shares): $4.65
Average share price ($25/5 purchases): $5.00

As you can see, not only does dollar-cost averaging work in any market environment, it also works for any type of investor with any amount of money to invest.

If you don't have much to invest, dollar-cost averaging can be a great way to ease into investing because you can start with a relatively small amount of money.

And if you have a large sum to invest (such as an inheritance), you can put the money into a savings or money market account, then move small portions into a stock or bond mutual fund over time.

And that's it. You're on your way to growing your portfolio with after-tax money—step 1. Well done! Now let's look at step 2.

Step 2: Pay Off Debt

Paying off debt is as important as anything you can do to put yourself in the best possible position for a secure retirement—and to achieve it, you'll need to figure out how much you owe and when you will be debt free if you keep making the same payments you're currently making.

To make this determination, there are many free debt calculators online. My favorite is Bankrate.com. Try it, then consider this:

If your debt is paid off prior to your projected retirement date, that's great. Keep doing what you're doing.

But if your debt payment extends into your retirement, then you *must* do one of two things: either increase your monthly debt payments, or push your retirement date off until your debt is paid off.

As I always say, *you can't retire until your debt retires.*

Step 3: Save Your Age Divided by Three

As a practicing economist for more than thirty-five years, I've looked at every possible way to advise my readers about the easiest and most accurate way to figure out how much money they should save for their retirement.

For clarity, when I refer to saving for retirement, I mean saving enough money to live essentially the same lifestyle after retirement as you did before retirement—not 80% of your current income, as some advisors will tell you. You don't want to cut back.

I can't tell you how upset I get when I walk into Walmart, Target, or McDonalds and see older folks working physically demanding jobs. I understand that some people just love to work, and need to stay busy. I understand that others look at the paycheck they receive from such jobs a way to cover some fun extras in their life. But I believe the majority of retirees would rather be home with their spouses, children, grandchildren, and even great-grandchildren than working near-minimum-wage jobs.

So when I see that happening, I wonder, what went wrong in those folks' lives to put them in the position to have to work those jobs?

I would love to sit down, buy them a cup of coffee, and listen to their story, but I'm pretty sure most of them would tell me the same thing—that they had no idea that retirement would sneak up on them so fast, and that they didn't know how much to save for the future.

Don't want that to be you? Well, I can't slow down time, but I can tell you how to calculate exactly how much you'll need to save to put yourself in the best possible position for a comfortable retirement. Are you ready?

Here it is. Don't blink or you'll miss it, because it's simple.

Take your age, divide it by three, and save that percentage of your gross salary.

That's it. That's the secret sauce.

Don't believe me? Here's an example.

Let's look at a twenty-five-year-old woman (I know, you likely aren't that young, but this is just an example. You'll see why I used a young age shortly.)

This young woman earns the median US salary of $59,039. Her age divided by three is 8.33%, and 8.33% of $59,039 is $4,918. So she'll need to save $4,918 per year to get on the path to secure retirement.

Don't believe me? By age sixty-five, this twenty-five-year-old woman will accumulate enough assets to create an income stream of $73,537. Add this to the median Social Security benefit for a sixty-five-year-old individual—$16,848 annually—and this saver will have a gross annual income of $90,385, which is $59,039, adjusted for inflation. (That means $87,331 gives this saver the same buying power as $59,039 did when she was twenty-five).

Now, let's look at another saver, a thirty-five-year-old man who waited until he was thirty-five to start saving for retirement. He also earns the median US salary of $59,039.

If you're like most of my readers, you probably think thirty-five is relatively young to begin saving for retirement. And it is. But this young man will pay a procrastination penalty for waiting those ten years.

The penalty is easy to determine. Start with age thirty-five and divide it by three, which gives us 11.67%. Since the age is higher, the percentage this young man must save is also higher.

You may think that's not too bad. This young man waited ten whole years to start saving, and he only has to save about 3% more than he would had he started at age twenty-five.

But this is where the majority of Americans make a fatal error that causes them to be working well into their seventies and eighties. They don't account for the procrastination penalty.

What is the procrastination penalty? It's the 8.33% this young man should have started saving at twenty-five. He has to add this percentage to his current savings rate of 11.67%, meaning he has to save roughly 20% of his gross annual income. That's quite a penalty!

And it compounds. Taking it a step further, a forty-five-year old woman who just started saving for retirement would have to save 15% of her gross income, plus the 11.67% she should have started saving at age thirty-five, plus the 8.333% she should have started saving at age twenty-five. That's roughly 35% of her gross income!

It's a tough pill to swallow, but if you do this, and earn a competitive return on your savings, in thirty years you'll be shopping at Macy's instead of working at Walmart.

I realize everyone reading this chapter knows that the longer you wait to save, the longer you have to save. What I'm hoping to accomplish here is to lay out, in simple mathematical terms, how much waiting actually costs you.

Try this calculation for your age; you'll see that it works.

My hope is that this doesn't discourage older Americans from saving because they can't reach their goals. Anything you can save today will make your life better tomorrow. But aim high—aim for your retirement GPS, which, in summary, is this:

Step 1: **G**row your portfolio after taxes.
Step 2: **P**ay off debt.
Step 3: **S**ave your age divided by three.

That's all there is to it. There's no magic. If you follow these steps, you'll achieve lowest-tax, most secure retirement possible.

That's what the rich do. They don't have 401(k) plans; they create all of their wealth with after-tax dollars.

As a sidenote, they then take advantage of the extremely attractive capital gains tax rate, and they pass their wealth to the next generation virtually tax free using the step up in cost basis. I know those are some new ideas, and I'll explain them all later.

For now, however, just remember this: If you think the tax system is tilted in favor of the rich, just remember who created it—the rich. And as long as the rich use their wealth to gain and keep power, that will never change. And if the system will never change, the only thing that can change is you.

Chapter VII

Don't Retire until your Debt is...

Pay Off Your Debt

> *Compound interest* is the eighth wonder of the world. He who understands it, earns it...He who doesn't...pays it. *Compound interest* is the most powerful force in the universe.
>
> —Albert Einstein

Debt. Almost everyone has it, but no one wants to talk about it.

It's time we do, so in this chapter I'm going to address the single biggest problem that stands between you and your freedom: debt.

According to figures from the New York Federal Reserve, total US consumer debt, which includes mortgages, auto loans, student loans, and credit cards, climbed to its highest level since 2010 in the third quarter of 2015. It stands at $12.07 trillion.

The average US household with debt now carries $129,579 in total debt, according to the 2015 American Household Credit Card Debt Study by NerdWallet, which analyzed data from several sources, including the New York Federal Reserve and the US Census Bureau, then commissioned an online survey of more than two thousand adults.

Total Debt Owed by US Consumers

Credit cards	$15,355
Mortgages	$165,892
Auto loans	$26,530
Student loans	$47,712
Any type of debt	$129,579

Source: 2015 American Household Credit Card Debt Study, Nerdwallet, as of Q3 2015.

How you think about these numbers isn't likely to be the same way your neighbor thinks about these numbers. That's because debt means different things to different people. Some say you need to borrow some gold to get to the pot of gold at the end of the rainbow. Some say it's a sign of failure. Others don't think of it at all. "What's the big deal?" they ask.

All of these perspectives may be accurate. In the right circumstances, debt can be helpful. A student loan can lead to a higher-paying job, for example, and a mortgage can ultimately allow one to reduce one's housing expenses. But not all debt is created equal. Credit card debt—and other debt with high interest rates—can be costly over the long term. The average household is paying a total of $6,658 in interest per year, according to Nerdwallet—9% of the average household income of $75,591.

To this economist, debt is the ultimate retirement killer. To show you what I mean, let's use an imaginary fellow named Allen as an example. Allen is reasonably intelligent. He works hard at a steady job that pays $3,000 per month after taxes. Thinking he deserves a break, Allen decides to take a European vacation. He pays for the vacation, which costs $5,000, with a credit card that charges 15% annual interest.

Off he goes. In Europe, Allen has a great time and buys numerous presents for his friends and family, spending an additional $1,000—so when he gets his credit card bill a few weeks after the trip, Allen owes $6,000. But this isn't unexpected, or even problematic. After all, Allen budgeted for this trip, and planned to pay off the credit card immediately with his savings when the bill came in.

What Allen didn't plan for was his car breaking down and his laptop needing repair. All the money he earmarked for his European vacation went to those expenses instead. So when Allen got the credit card bill for his vacation, he couldn't pay it.

"Never mind," thought Allen. "I'll pay the minimum this month, and the balance in full next month." What do you think happened? You guessed it. Next month Allen's niece got married, and Allen needed to buy a new suit and cover travel expenses for the out-of-town wedding. Again, he made the minimum payment and promised himself he'd pay the balance in full next month.

Eventually, Allen gives up waiting for next month to come and just keeps paying the minimum, long after the memories of the vacation have faded away.

I realize this is nothing new. We've all fallen victim to the way life gets in the way of our plans. But few of us think of the true cost, numerically speaking.

Let's see what the true cost is of Allan's vacation. If he pays $100 per month on a $6,000 credit card bill at 15%, it would take him 111 months to pay off the balance in full. The total cost would be $11,100—or, 3.7 months of work, and that doesn't even include taxes. So that one-week vacation pushed back Allan's retirement almost four months! I hope he had fun.

With that as a backdrop, let's take a look at different types of debt, and consider how an economist views them. First up: mortgages.

How Much Is Debt Costing You?

It depends. But consider that auto buyers with fair credit will end up spending about six times more to finance a vehicle than buyers with excellent credit, according to WalletHub's 2015 Auto Financing Report. That equates to $6,100 in additional interest payments over the life of a $20,000, five-year loan.

The Best Debt: Mortgages

When we think of debt, many of us first think of mortgages, because they're often the largest part of our household debt. And mortgage debt is growing, as if we learned nothing from the financial crisis. It surged $144 billion in the third quarter of 2015, according to the New York Federal Reserve, marking the second biggest rise since 2007—when we were in a housing bubble, if you recall.

I won't bore you with a lecture about what a mortgage is. I figure if you're reading this book, you already know what one is, and most likely have one.

I'll just note that mortgages are indispensable economic tools. They form the backbone of any civilized society. Indeed, the economic impact of mortgages is so immense, it's virtually immeasurable. So you won't be surprised to hear me say that in my opinion, a mortgage is one of the best kinds of debt. Yes, there are problems with mortgages, and I'll address them later in this chapter. But for now, look at a mortgage this way.

Jill and Jane buy a house for $220,000. They put down the traditional 10%, which is $20,000, and secure a thirty-year, fixed-rate mortgage at the current rate of 3.50% for the remaining $280,000. Their mortgage looks like this:

Mortgage Repayment Summary

Amount borrowed: $280,000
Payoff date: February 2045
Total payments: 360
Monthly payment amount: $898.09
Total of 360 payments: $323,312.18
Total interest paid: $123,312.18

Some of you might say the monthly cost should be higher due to real-estate taxes. Others might say it should be lower due to income-tax deductions. I'm intentionally not incorporating real-estate taxes and income-tax deductions in this scenario for good reason: I don't want this to be an accounting class, but a demonstration of how one can look at things differently.

The number that stands out to most people is the total interest paid during the term of the mortgage: $123,312.18. Since there has never been a thirty-year period in the history of this country where real estate didn't appreciate, I think it is safe to assume that Jill and Jane's home will be worth at least the purchase price of $220,000. So the interest is what it cost them to "rent" their home all those years. With that in mind, let's do some quick math. The interest of $123,312.18 divided by 360 months equals $342.53 per month. That means that Jill and Jane lived in the house for $342.53 per month for 30 years. If that is less expensive than renting the same house, buying the home is a good deal. (Again, I know we didn't include real-estate taxes in our calculation, nor did we factor in homeowners' insurance and repairs. But if we assume the value of the house over thirty years simply keeps up with inflation, we have those expenses covered.)

A Trip Back in Time

So far, then, mortgages make sense. But what happened to mortgage debt during the Great Recession? I wrote about it in *The Money Compass*, noting that I first predicted impending doom in March 2006. "In the next five years, house values are going to return to their 1997 levels plus inflation," I wrote. "Inflation since 1997 is roughly 21%. That means to calculate the value of your house in 2011, take the 1997 value and add 21%. For most of us, that is quite an adjustment from 2006 values."

I again discussed it in January 2007. "A new wave of mortgage defaults is imminent—a situation which would flood the housing market with an even greater supply of unsold homes and potentially weakens the U.S. economy as a whole," I wrote. "Home prices will continue to fall."

Then it happened. Essentially, the housing market fell apart as two economic situations combined to create what many economists consider the perfect storm. First, interest rates began to rise, and second, housing prices began to weaken. Troubled borrowers had only one choice, and foreclosures on subprime loans started to rise.

Initially, the federal government insisted that the problem was contained. On June 5, 2007, Federal Reserve President Ben Bernanke told a South African audience that "troubles in the subprime sector seem unlikely to seriously spill over to the broader economy or the financial system."

That clearly wasn't true, however. As early as March 2007, the entire housing market was suffering, with national home sales and prices seeing dramatic declines. Existing-home sales were down 13% from their peak of 554,000 in March 2006 to 482,000 a year later, the steepest since 1989. Meanwhile, the national median price of existing homes had fallen 6% from a peak of $230,200 in July 2006 to $217,000 a year later.

If the problem had been limited just to the housing market, there might have been a quick resolution. But this housing-market correction was like no other in that it led to a crisis of confidence in the global banking system.

For example, in July, Bear Stearns & Co. disclosed that two of its hedge funds, which had bet heavily on securities tied to subprime mortgages, had lost nearly all of their value.

When Germany's IKB Deutsche Industriebank announced major subprime losses as well, forcing the German government to organize a €3.5-billion bailout in August 2007, the world began to worry.

Then, on August 9, 2007, French bank BNP Paribas announced that it wouldn't allow investors to withdraw money from three funds because it couldn't determine the market for their holdings. "The complete evaporation of liquidity in certain market segments of the U.S. securitization market has made it impossible to value certain assets fairly regardless of their quality or credit rating," the bank said. In other words, banks didn't know what mortgage-backed securities holding subprime mortgages were worth, due to the tranches, and since no one was buying them, there was no market price.

As fear paralyzed the world credit markets, the world's central bankers responded. The European Central Bank (ECB) was the first to act, with an injection €94.8 billion into European money markets, a larger infusion than the one that came after the September

11 terrorist attacks. Other central banks followed with similar, but smaller steps. The Fed, for example, injected $38 billion into the money markets, but not in a traditional fashion. The Fed, which usually buys US Treasuries, bought bonds backed by subprime mortgages, because there were so few buyers for them. In essence, the Fed became the buyer of last resort.

In the following weeks, the Fed, for its part, followed the traditional playbook to some extent. On August 17, 2007, one week after the credit crunch first surfaced, the Fed lowered its discount rate (which it charges qualified lenders for temporary loans) from 6.25% to 5.75%. In a slightly more unusual move, the Fed also extended the duration on loans banks took out under the discount window, which is the facility through which the Fed makes loans to commercial banks (which pledge a variety of financial instruments as collateral), from overnight to thirty days.

On August 31, 2007, President Bush tried to intervene, outlining a plan that would help troubled subprime borrowers keep their homes via changes to the Federal Housing Administration (FHA) mortgage insurance program. Those changes would allow more people to refinance with FHA insurance if they were to fall behind on adjustable-rate mortgages, which offer low introductory rates that can later rise, sometimes doubling a monthly payment. White House officials estimated the initiative could help as many as eighty thousand new homeowners—which, interestingly, is the exact number of homeowners who were able to initially buy new homes thanks to the earlier passed American Dream Down Payment Initiative.

At first these moves were well received, with the US equity markets rallying to new highs in the following weeks. Still, tight credit conditions would not abate, so the Fed persisted, and soon showed it was willing to get aggressive if necessary. On September 18, the central bank cut both the discount rate and the federal funds rate, to 5.25% and 4.75%, respectively.

By the end of 2007, the discount rate was at 4.75% and the federal funds rate was at 4.25%, but it was clear these low interest rates wouldn't be the easy fix they were in the past. Some analysts said this was because the Fed hadn't responded quickly enough, but the medicine still didn't match the illness. It was impossible to value—and thus trade—banks' assets. By December 2007, the Fed understood, and, in coordination with other world central banks, announced a surprise two-part plan to combat the credit crunch by pumping money into the global banking system.

First, the Fed, along with the ECB, Bank of Canada, Bank of England, and Swiss National Bank, created a new lending facility called a term auction facility. This was a hybrid of the Fed's two normal funding methods of auctioning of funds to twenty-one primary dealers via a system of repurchase agreements, and the discount window available to commercial banks.[1] Under the term auction facility, the Fed auctioned off funds, but any commercial bank deemed to be in generally sound financial condition by its local Fed bank could participate (anonymously, and by pledging a wider variety of financial instruments as collateral).

Second, the Fed set up $20 billion swap lines with the ECB and $4 billion swap lines with the Swiss National Bank. Under these swap lines, the Fed agreed to loan the central banks a total of $24 billion, which the banks could in turn lend to commercial banks in Europe.[2] This, it reasoned, would help large commercial banks in foreign countries gain access to US dollars.

By then, the housing market was in dire straits. Sales of existing single-family homes fell in 2007 by 13%, the largest amount in twenty-five years. At the same time, the median home price dropped 1.8% to $217,000, the first annual price decline on record, which goes back to 1968. Lawrence Yuan, the chief economist at the

---

1 Repurchase agreements, or repos, occur when securities are sold with the stipulation that they will be repurchased at a later date at a higher price. The increase is the interest paid by the seller of the securities to the purchaser of the securities. The purpose of such an agreement is to provide the seller with cash, and it is essentially a loan initiated by the seller. In the case of the Fed, the repurchasing plan was an attempt to put more cash into the economy as credit was drying up during the meltdown.

2 Swap lines are used to increase US dollars available to foreign central banks. They are swaps between US dollar and foreign currencies. The foreign central banks use the US dollars to ease credit restrictions, i.e., increase liquidity, in their countries to help prevent financial problems from occurring in these regions.

National Association of Realtors, said it was likely that the country had not experienced such a decline in housing prices since the Great Depression.

We didn't know it then, but by the end of the year, the US economy was already in a recession that came to be called the Great Recession.

Even at the time, I knew what the central banks had done wasn't enough. "I believe the worst is yet to come," I wrote in February 2008. "Why? Because unlike many other corrections (1987, 1997, 1998, 2001 and 2002), this time American homeowners have their biggest assets on the table, their houses."

We have *The Money Compass* to thank for the look back at history. Now let's build on what we wrote. If mortgages are indeed the best kind of debt to have, why did the housing-market depression happen? It's really very simple. Millions of hardworking Americans bought the same house over and over again.

How is that possible? Because every time you refinance your house, you purchase it from yourself at a higher and higher price. And even worse, you started the thirty-year amortization clock from the beginning.

Let me say that again. If you bought a home for $175,000 in 2004, refinanced it for $225,000 in 2005, and refinanced it again for $250,000 in 2007, each time you increased the true purchase price. But just as bad, with each refinance you also pushed back your payoff date, thus pushing back your retirement. (As I always like to say, "Don't retire until your debt is.") This has left millions of American to "spend" their retirements in their forties and fifties.

The Devil in Your Wallet

We've talked about mortgages, with an aside about retirement, so now I'd like to talk about how to manage your credit card debt.

Credit card debt has been an important part of the rise in household debt, but how much depends on how you define credit cards and count the card-carrying population. For example, you might exclude transactors, who pay off their credit card balances each month. Just to give you an idea, however, NerdWallet says each US household with debt carries an average of $15,355 in credit card debt.

We also know that over the long term, the average amount credit card debt has steadily risen. An individual born between 1980 and 1984 has $5,689 more in credit card debt than one born between 1950 and 1954 (i.e., his or her parents) at the same stage of life and $8,156 more than one born between 1920 and 1924 (i.e., his or her grandparents), according to "New Evidence on Credit Card Borrowing and Repayment Patterns," published in Economic Inquiry in January 2013.

Now, as is the case with a mortgage, life for most of us would be extremely difficult without at least one major credit card. So I'll spare you the "never use a credit card" lecture. Instead, let's talk about how to best manage your use of credit cards.

The main advantage of using a credit card is that it builds your credit history. Responsible usage will help increase your credit score, and the higher your credit score, the lower the interest rate lenders will charge you.

The disadvantages of credit cards, however, are significant. For example, I'm truly amazed that even the most cost-conscious consumer will totally disregard the cost the cards add to every purchase. That's because if you're like most consumers, and you carry a balance from month to month, credit cards increase the true cost of every item you purchase with them. That means that the cost of your purchase will continue to grow month after month after month. A $175 jacket could end up costing you $500—and the only reason you bought it was because it was marked down from $200. You thought $200 was too much to pay for the jacket, but in the end, it cost you $500. That is called revolving credit, and it's cancer to your financial life.

Here are some rules to live by when it comes to credit cards.

1. Let's face it; life in this century requires a major credit card. But if you must have one, get one that has a low annual fee.
2. Use the card responsibly.

3. Using the card a little is better than not using it at all. Creditors want to see that you can manage your usage. They like the Goldilocks creditors—not too much usage, and not too little. Let's beat them at their own game. Put no more than five hours of your monthly income on the card each month. So if you make $20 an hour, then put $100 on the card each month. Then pay it in full. By doing this, your FICO score will increase, thus reducing the interest you're charged.
4. If you can't pay the full balance at the end of the month, then pay the most you can on the card with the highest interest rate first.
5. If you carry a balance from month to month, you need to stop using the card—period. No dinners out, no new clothes, no weekends away. No new charges period. Not even $1.60 for a candy bar. If you carry a balance you are tapped out—and carrying a balance is the same as lighting the debt fuse. Trust me, that fuse can lead to a complete destruction of the golden years.

How to Fix Your High Credit Card Balance

1. Stop using your credit cards.
2. Pay off the cards with the highest interest rates first.
3. Stop saving money, and put all that money toward debt. Even your 401(k). Stop depositing money above the company match, and put that money toward debt.
4. Have a garage sale and put all that money toward debt.
5. Reduce your expenses as much as possible and put all that money toward debt.

How Not to Fix Your High Credit Card Balance

1. Do not pull money from your retirement account.
2. Do not take out a consolidation loan. If you do, you will only run up the cards again before the loan is paid off. Trust me, I have seen it hundreds of times.

Car, Shmar

Full disclosure: I'm a car guy. I love them. All types and styles. New and old. Fast and faster.

And some cars can be investments. I learned many years ago that there are two very different car worlds—the retail world, which consists of all the neighborhood cars, including the Honda Accords, Toyota Highlanders, Ford Explorers, and Jeep Wranglers, and the classic car world. I'm fascinated by both worlds, and I have cars that fall into both categories. While both worlds are driven economically by supply and demand, retail cars offer much more to the consumer. They're newer, they're safer, and they come with a warranty. The classic cars are usually very old, have almost no safety features, and aren't very reliable. Yet in almost all cases the classic car will appreciate.

But, chances are, you have (and need) a retail car, as do most Americans. And you'll probably need a loan to buy one.

Auto loans are also a growing part of consumer debt. They climbed for the eighteenth straight time in the third quarter of 2015, according to the New York Federal Reserve, rising by $39 billion to $1.05 trillion, the biggest increase since 2005. And many consumers are financing their purchases for longer terms. In the middle of 2015 the average loan length for a new car was sixty-seven months, and for a used car sixty-two months, according to Experian.

So let's set some guidelines to follow when you purchase your next retail car to reduce that depreciation as much as possible.

1. Buy what you can afford, not what you deserve.
2. Buy a car that is two to three years old. Much of the depreciation occurs during the first three years, so it makes sense to buy a car after that happens.
3. Find a car that has fewer than thirty-six thousand miles on it. Most factory warranties last for three years and/or thirty-six thousand miles.
4. Try to pay cash for the car. If you can't, don't finance it for more than three years.
5. Try to keep the car for six years. If so, you will have three years of no payment, and after six years the car should still

have enough value to provide a 15% to 20% down payment on your next car.

Student Loans: The Simmering Volcano

And any discussion of debt wouldn't be complete without mentioning student loans. They hit a new record of $1.2 trillion in the third quarter of 2015, according to the New York Federal Reserve. And the delinquency rate on student debt rose for the second straight quarter to 11.6%. In fact, at the end of 2014, only 37% of all 43.3 million student-loan borrowers nationwide were making payments on time and reducing their loan balances.

Debt: America's Dirty Secret

Why is debt growing so dramatically? One reason is that the growth in the cost of living has outpaced income growth. Since 2003, median household income has grown 26% while the cost of living has grown 29%, according to Nerdwallet. While 3% may not seem like a significant difference, it's more for those in certain groups—for example, those who have chronic health problems, as medical costs have grown by 51% since 2013.

There's also been a change in the way we think about debt. When I was growing up, people bought cars for cash, and sometimes houses too. Today, you can get a thirty-five-year mortgage, something that would have been unheard of not long ago. We're assuming debt is normal, and as a result, we aren't thinking about it very much. As a result, we're glossing over how much we have. According to Nerdwallet, as of 2013, actual lender-reported credit card debt was 155% greater than borrower-reported balances. We're also not understanding how debt works. According to Bankrate.com, 77% of Americans don't know that credit card accounts with high outstanding balances hurt their credit scores, even if they pay the bills on time. More than half think carrying a balance can improve their credit scores.

For many, getting out of debt requires a new perspective. Many Americans live their entire lives in debt. They like shiny new things. So they buy bigger and better houses. (When's the last time you heard of someone paying off a mortgage?) When they pay off one car loan, they get another.

I Can Guess Your Retirement Date

Debt is important because most people spend their retirement before it even begins.

Let me explain. Whenever I speak to a large audience, the subject of retirement always comes up—because if there's one thing almost all Americans can agree on, it's that retirement scares us to death. Most of us feel like we won't be able to retire at all, let alone retire comfortably.

I like to play a little trick to get my audience to truly understand how important debt is in their lives. I tell them I can see into the future, and predict the exact day that they could retire if they wanted to. I ask for volunteers, and a couple of dozen hands always go up. I always pick a baby boomer, thank him or her for participating, and explain that I will only need to know the answer to one question before my magic powers of economics kicks in and I provide the answer to the seemingly impossible question of "When will I be able to retire?"

The question is "Tell me the date you will be debt free."

If the participant says he or she will not be debt free for another twenty years, I explain that debt is nothing more than wages we haven't earned yet, so he or she better keep on working.

Debt, in my opinion, is the single biggest determining factor in forecasting one's retirement. That's because debt is guaranteed to keep growing each and every day.

And what's worse is that the interest is compounding, meaning that you pay interest on interest. As Albert Einstein once said, "Compounding interest is the greatest force in the universe."

The question is how do you take that force and make it work for you instead of against you? Well, you begin by paying off your debt as quickly and painlessly as possible.

Here's my challenge to you: stop the cycle. Debt turns you into a slave, forcing you to toil away, hour and hour, just to meet its demands. Each month, you feel farther and farther behind, like all your hard work was for nothing. Reducing it will greatly reduce the risk in your life, and let you lead one of safety and balance.

Start with the debt that has the highest interest rates first. That doesn't mean you wipe out your emergency fund. Here's what I do. I analyze my debt and determine what my debt-free date would be if I keep making the same payments. If that date is past the date on which I'd like to retire, I had better redo my budget and find some more cash to apply to what I owe—even if that means cutting vacations, dining out, and even college savings. Nothing should come between you and being debt free before your retirement. On the other hand, if I do that calculation and discover I will be debt free prior to my planned retirement, then my cash flow is fine and I can spend a little or save a little.

Paying down your debt is the only true guaranteed investment you will ever make. It's also the only path to a secure retirement. So go ahead and write down all your debt and use one of the many online calculators to figure out when you'll be debt free. Write the date on a Post-it note and put on your refrigerator.

I suggest you update the number every six months. If the date keeps moving out into the future, you'll see the true cost of some of those things you purchased that you couldn't afford. Those items may have seemed inexpensive and necessary at the time, but all they really did was shorten your long-awaited and well-earned retirement years.

Chapter VIII

Uncle Sam's Slight of Hand...

Retirement, Then and Now: Rise of the 401(k) Plan

401(k) plans are the foundation of many Americans' retirement savings—but they're relatively new, and came into existence, some would say, by coincidence. Let's take a look back through time to gain a better understanding of how 401(k) plans came about and why they're so popular.

401(k) Basics

First, let's cover the basics. A 401(k) plan is a tax-qualified, defined-contribution pension plan. Under these plans, contributions are deducted from an employee's paycheck before taxation; these contributions may also be proportionately matched by an employer. The benefit: contributions (and earnings) are tax-deferred until withdrawn after the employee reaches retirement age (or is otherwise permitted to make a withdrawal under the law—we'll get into that later). Annual contribution limits are $18,000 in 2016, which means you can reduce your current taxable income significantly by investing in a 401(k) plan. And when you do pay taxes on that money, you'll hopefully be in a lower tax bracket, because you'll be retired.

<<Other employer-provided defined-contribution plans include 403(b) plans, which cater to employees of nonprofit institutions, and 457(b) plans, which cater to employees of government institutions.>>

History of the 401(k)

In order to understand today's 401(k) plans, it helps to have an understanding of how the defined-contribution industry has evolved.

Before 1978, deferred compensation arrangements were being used by some companies to allow employee compensation (and the resulting tax liability) to be deferred. Usually, those employees were executives. In the early 1970s, Congress began debating the propriety of this favorable treatment. The problem, as they saw it, was that executives at some companies were getting perks (in the ability to defer taxes) the mainstream public was not.

Ultimately, the lawmakers ended up creating the Revenue Act of 1978, which inserted a provision into the Internal Revenue Code. This provision, subsection 401(k), allowed employees to avoid being taxed on the portion of income that they decided to receive as deferred compensation rather than direct pay.

Congress never intended to create the 401(k) industry as we know it today. Indeed, subsection 401(k) was intended to be a minor clarification, affecting only a handful of companies that used deferred compensation arrangements. But as it turned out, someone figured out that subsection 401(k) could be extended to cover a multitude of retirement plans.

It is widely believed that someone was Ted Benna, a benefits consultant. In 1980, as the story is told, Benna interpreted the law to create a 401(k) plan for his employer, a Philadelphia-based benefits consultancy called the Johnson Companies. That plan Benna created looked a lot like today's 401(k) plan: it allowed employees to fund retirement accounts using pretax dollars, with the company matching contributions.

It would be hard to understate what a novel idea this was. Today, we take for granted the ability to squirrel away pretax earnings, with a company match to boot. At the time, however, it seemed unlikely that Benna's idea would hold up under Internal Revenue Service (IRS) scrutiny. "I had only one thought at the time," Benna told MarketWatch. "How could I make this sucker fly?"

Perhaps the biggest hurdle was that the IRS had to formally allow employees to put money into 401(k) plans by reducing their wages. And in 1981, the IRS issued rules doing just that—allowing the funding of 401(k) plans through employee salary reductions.

Still, Benna recalls that even with IRS approval, many pension consulting firms considered the concept a scam. But that same year, according to the Employee Benefits Research Institute (EBRI), several companies—including Hughes Aircraft Company, Johnson & Johnson, PepsiCo, JC Penney, and Honeywell—developed proposals for 401(k) plans. Soon those plans were up and running. On January 25, 1982, a *Wall Street Journal* article stated, "If the boss suggests you take a pay cut, don't panic. The company may be offering you the chance at a tax-sheltered savings program that is even better than an Individual Retirement Account."

Over the years, the rules were modified. For example, the Tax Reform Act of 1984 required nondiscrimination testing to ensure that contributions to 401(k) plans didn't discriminate in favor of highly compensated employees by more than an allowable amount. (Congress was concerned that wealthy executives would take advantage of 401(k) plans more than lower-paid employees.) But essentially, by 1981, the modern 401(k) plan had been born.

At the time, there was no indication that 401(k) plans would become the pillar of the American retirement system as they are today. But corporate America had a motivation to make them popular: by implementing a tax-sheltered retirement system, companies could shed their pension responsibilities. And, employees benefited, too, with the tax deferral. Remember, back then the top marginal income tax rate was 70%. The 401(k) plan allowed one to defer taxes on a portion of one's income until retirement, when likely in a much lower tax bracket.

At first, 401(k) plans were only available at a handful of large companies, such as those mentioned above. But the idea quickly took off, and according to the EBRI, citing US Department of Labor Form 5500 reports, by 1984 there were 17,303 plans with a 401(k) feature. These plans had 7,540,000 active participants and assets of $91.75 billion. By 1990, all three numbers had skyrocketed. There were 97,614 plans with a 401(k) feature; 19,548,000 active participants; and $384.85 billion in assets. And by 1996, there were 230,808 plans with a 401(k) feature; 30,843,000 active participants; and $1.06 trillion in assets.

"I knew it was going to be big, but I was certainly not anticipating that it would be the primary way people would be accumulating money for retirement 30-plus years later," Benna told Workforce magazine.

<<When conceived by Congress, 401(k) plans were expected to have a negligible effect on tax revenue. By 2013, that effect was an estimated $57 billion—equal, according to Morningstar, to the combined costs of running the departments of the Treasury, the Interior, and Labor; the Army Corps of Engineers; the Social Security Administration; the National Science Foundation; and the Small Business Administration.>>

Turning Points

Since then, there have been some major changes in laws affecting 401(k) plans, the first being the Economic Growth and Tax Relief Reconciliation Act of 2001. This act provided for catch-up contributions and the Roth 401(k).

Catch-up contributions allow 401(k) plan participants fifty and older to make larger contributions than everyone else—an additional $6,000 in 2016. The idea: help those Americans who are approaching retirement and haven't saved enough get caught up.

Roth 401(k) plans combine the advantages of the Roth Individual Retirement Account with the 401(k) plan. With a Roth 401(k), employees may choose to contribute funds to their retirement accounts on an *after-tax* basis. In other words, with a Roth 401(k), you use money from your paycheck after it has already been taxed. The benefit: at retirement, qualified withdrawals are tax free. This may appeal to individuals who expect to be in a higher tax bracket at retirement.

Another turning point was the Pension Protection Act of 2006, which allowed employers to automatically enroll employees in 401(k) plans. As previously mentioned, when initially conceived, 401(k) plans weren't intended to be Americans' primary retirement-savings vehicles. As it became clear they would be, policymakers became concerned that not enough people were enrolled and stashing money away. The industry responded with automatic-enrollment programs, which allow companies to place new employees into a plan and a default investment (often a target-date fund). Employees can always opt out, but often don't.

<<According to Vanguard research, 401(k) plans with voluntary enrollment see a 42% participation rate, while plans with automatic enrollment see a 91% participation rate.>>

The Big Benefit: Tax Deferral

As already touched upon, the major benefit of the 401(k) plan is tax deferral. Contributions can be made with either pretax or after-tax contributions.

On pretax contributions (which can total up to $18,000 in 2016, as noted), the employee does not pay federal income tax. As an example, consider a single individual who earns $100,000 in a particular year, has one exemption, and no other adjustments (such as deductions). According to online calculator Financial Finesse, he or she would normally pay $18,184 in federal income tax. If that employee contributed $18,000 to a 401(k) account on a pretax basis, however, he or she would only report $88,000 in income on that year's tax return, and pay just $13,684 in federal income taxes. That's $4,500 in taxes saved. The money in the account grows (depending on the performance of the investments) tax deferred. At the time of withdrawal, the pretax contributions and earnings on it are taxed as ordinary income.

Employees can also make after-tax contributions to a non–Roth 401(k) plan (up to a limit—in 2016, the total 401(k) plan contribution cannot exceed $53,000). Why? Perhaps the employee wants to contribute more than the pretax limit of $18,000, and enjoy tax-deferred compounding on those after-tax contributions. In this case, contributions aren't taxed when withdrawn (because they've already been taxed), and earnings are taxed as ordinary income.

Note that to maintain the tax advantage for income deferred into a 401(k), money must be kept in the plan until the employee reaches age fifty-nine and a half. Money withdrawn prior to that time typically incurs a 10% penalty tax on top of the ordinary income tax that has to be paid on a withdrawal.

There are a few exceptions to the 10% penalty, however; they are listed in Section 72(t)(2) of the Internal Revenue Code. Some are obvious: the employee's death, for example, or the employee's total and permanent disability. Others are also fairly easy to understand: the use of the funds for deductible medical expenses exceeding the 7.5% of adjusted gross income, or to maintain compliance with a qualified domestic relations order. Others are more complex, however. For example, another exception to the penalty occurs if the employee separates from service with the employer maintaining the plan during or after the year the employee reaches age fifty-five. And, there is an exception if distributions are made as part of a series of substantially equal periodic payments over the employee's life expectancy (or the life expectancies of the employee and a designated beneficiary), and the employee separates from service with the employer maintaining the plan before the payments begin for this exception to apply.

Flexibility

Another advantage of 401(k) plans is the flexibility they offer employees, both when working for the employer offering the plan and after separating from service.

For example, many 401(k) plans allow employees to take loans from their plans at predefined interest rates; the employee then repays the loans from his or her paycheck. So the employee is actually paying himself or herself interest, instead of a bank. There are rules surrounding loans—for example, the loan term cannot be longer than five years (except in the case of the purchase of a primary residence). And if an employee does not make payments in accordance with the rules, the outstanding loan balance is declared in default, and becomes a taxable distribution to the employee.

The ability to roll funds from a 401(k) plan to another defined-contribution plan (such as another 401(k) plan or an IRA) is also appealing to many investors, especially those who change jobs. Rollovers can be made directly from plan to plan, or by a distribution to the participant and a subsequent rollover to another plan. Again, there are some rules—for example, rollovers must generally be accomplished within sixty days of the distribution.

Finally, 401(k) plans also allow for hardship withdrawals without penalty. Hardships are defined by the IRS as unreimbursed medical expenses for the participant, the participant's spouse, or the participant's dependent; payment of college tuition and related educational costs for the participant, the participant's spouse or dependents, or children who are no longer dependents; payments necessary to prevent eviction from or foreclosure on the participant's home; and funeral expenses. Some employers may disallow some or all of these hardship causes, so you wouldn't want to assume you can take a hardship withdrawal without checking with your company.

Otherwise, while you remain in service of a company and are under the age of fifty-nine and a half, you may be able to get money you've contributed out of a 401(k) plan, but the distribution will be taxed as ordinary income and a 10% penalty will apply, if no exceptions are applicable.

<<401(k) Plans Today

Total value of assets held in 401(k) plans	$4.5 trillion
Percent of all retirement assets held in 401(k) plans	18%
Total number of 401(k) plan participants	52,500,000
Total number of 401(k) plans	515,000
Percentage of full time workers who have employee-sponsored 401(k) plans	78%
Percentage of workers who participate in their available 401(k) plans	81.5%
Average percent of salary contributed to a 401(k) plan	6.8%
Percent of 401(k) plan assets held in mutual funds	64%

Source: Statistic Brain, citing data from Independent Directors Council, Center for Retirement Research, Bureau of Labor Statistics, as of August 1, 2016.>>

Criticisms

One criticism of 401(k) plans is their required minimum distributions (RMDs). Participants must begin taking distributions from their accounts by April 1 of the calendar year after they turn age seventy and a half or April 1 of the calendar year after retiring, whichever is later. The distributions are based on life expectancy. These rules apply to pretax and after-tax contributions to a traditional 401(k) plan; Roth 401k plans are an exception. Failure to take a distribution can be high—50% of the amount that should have been distributed.

Fees have been another criticism of 401(k) plans. All 401(k) plans charge fees, for both administrative and investment management services. These fees can be charged to the employer, the plan participants, or to the plan itself, and the fees can be allocated in many ways. According to the Center for American Progress, the average 401(k) plan charges approximately 1% of assets managed in fees. And all told, the center estimates that a typical worker will be assessed a total of $138,336 in fees over his or her lifetime. That's a lot of cash to lose in fees.

Finally, some have questioned how effective 401(k) plans are. Even Benna, the so-called father of the 401(k), is no longer an unabashed fan. Although he believes the retirement-savings vehicles are benefiting millions of employees, he's concerned that they've become too complicated. He told MarketWatch he intended them to be as simple as traditional pension plans, with two investment options: a guaranteed fund and an equity fund. The guaranteed fund would guarantee you a minimum at retirement, and the equity fund would allow for a little more (or less, depending on performance). Most people, he said, would split their contributions equally between the two. Today, 401(k) plans have numerous investment options, from income to equities to alternatives, and Benna says that provides too many opportunities for mistakes. "We said, we are going to make people smart and savvy enough to make the right investment decisions, but it just hasn't worked," he told MarketWatch.

Chapter IX

You're the Target...

Target-Date Retirement Funds: The Lie Inside the Lie

A large problem is brewing in most Americans' 401(k). It's a problem that is hidden in plain sight by some very clever marketing. It's a problem so big that the only way to fix it is to break federal securities law. Wall Street knows about it, the US government knows about it, and now you, the target of the problem, will know about it.

The lie: "Set it and forget it" works.

In this chapter, I plan to expose target-date retirement funds as gimmicks whose popularity far overshoots their effectiveness. I will expose them as ticking time bombs (with misleading fees) that are actually acting counter to their intended purpose by adding risk as time goes by.

What Is a Target-Date Retirement Fund?

Very simply, a target-date retirement fund, also called a target-date fund, is a fund that automatically rebalances its holdings to become more conservative as an investor gets closer to retirement. These funds are designed for investors who prefer to put their portfolios on autopilot. They are perhaps the lowest-maintenance retirement-saving product you can purchase. And that's exactly what makes them so popular. With a target-date fund, you can set it and forget it, so to speak.

Who Do Target-Date Retirement Funds Target?

You, that's who.

Let me tell you a story about a woman, who wrote to me in 2013 about an experience she had investing in target-date funds, which, as I've noted, automatically rebalance their assets to become more conservative as an investor gets closer to retirement.

In 2005, Jane Doe, as I'll call her to protect her privacy, received a large inheritance from her parent's estate. Having no experience managing a six-figure portfolio, Jane asked for recommendations, and friends suggested she call one of the large national investment firms. Jane did so, speaking to a client-service representative who asked questions designed to determine Jane's investment experience, investment horizon, and tolerance for risk—much what you'd expect of any financial professional.

"At the time, I was 57 years old and I thought that this inheritance would put me on pace to retire at age 65," recalls Jane, a single mother and the sole breadwinner in her family, who had previously handled all of her own retirement planning, placing other investments in very conservative mutual funds.

The client service representative Jane spoke to told her that a target-date fund would be a fantastic choice, and explained why.

First, the target date, the client service representative explained, refers to a target retirement date, and often is part of the name of the fund. For example, you might see target-date funds with names such as Retirement 2030 Fund or Target 2030 Fund, which would be designed for individuals who intend to retire during or near the year 2030.

The client service representative also told Jane that target-date funds offer a long-term investment strategy based on holding a mix of stocks, bonds, and other investments that automatically shift as the participant ages. For example, a fund's initial asset allocation, when the target date is years away, might consist primarily of stocks, which have greater return potential but also greater volatility. As the target date approaches, the fund's asset allocation might shift to include a higher proportion of more conservative investments, such as bonds and cash, which generally are less volatile. "As a novice, I thought that this was a very prudent approach," says Jane.

That's a thought echoed by other purveyors of target-date funds. "They're an excellent investment solution for most people in most situations," said one financial planner at T. Rowe Price, which offers a full menu of target-date funds, quoted in the media. "I liken them to being the automatic transmission of the investing world—and 95% of cars sold in North America have automatic transmission."

Since Jane's desired retirement date was 2013, when she turned sixty-five, the client service representative recommended that Jane split the assets between two funds, one with a target retirement date of 2010 and one with a target retirement date of 2015. Jane agreed, and was thrilled with her decision. "When the call was finished, I was filled with confidence and was very proud of myself for selecting a combination of two funds that would be managed in accordance with my risk and retirement in mind," she says.

Jane's investment strategy worked well for a few years, but then the financial crisis hit. In 2008, the fund with a target retirement date of 2010 lost 20.67%, and the fund with a target retirement date of 2015 lost 24.06%. Jane was devastated and flabbergasted. "I couldn't believe that these funds didn't do what they were advertised to do," she says. "I couldn't sleep."

When Jane called the mutual fund company (several times) for an explanation, the client service representatives she spoke with simply told her to stay the course. Jane, however, wanted answers. "How could a fund with a retirement date of 2010 lose 20% just two years before its maturity date?" she asks. "I want to know, because I'm forced to postpone my retirement for at least two years as a result."

The Retirement Plans Role

Much of the growth in target-date funds is due to defined-contribution retirement plan assets invested in target-date strategies.

For the twelve months ended September 30, 2016, target-date funds took 18.4% of the $3.28 trillion total defined-contribution plan assets among the one thousand largest retirement plans, up from 16.8% in the prior period, according to *Pensions & Investments.*

All told, as of that date, target-date funds represented 17.7% of aggregate $1.96 trillion of assets among the top two hundred defined-contribution plans, up from 16.2% the year before.

These funds' potential for continued growth is so strong that Russell Investments predicts they could represent 70% of defined-contribution retirement plan assets in ten years.

That, in part, is because more and more defined-contribution retirement plans, such as 401(k) plans, are offering automatic enrollment. After the Pension Protection Act passed, target-date funds became eligible to be qualified default investment alternatives. Today, target-date funds are usually the default option when employers automatically enroll workers in 401(k) plans, and as of 2017 they can be found in nine out of ten workplace plans, according to Aon Hewitt. In other words, if you don't specify how you want your 401(k) plan assets invested, they will likely be invested in a target-date fund.

Here's another problem with target-date funds in retirement plans: the domination of the large 401(k) plan managers crowds out smaller (and possibly better) target-date funds. Think about it. If Vanguard manages your 401(k) plan, you're likely to be offered only Vanguard target-date funds, even if other target-date funds are better. It's like going to Walmart and only being able to buy Walmart-brand paper towels.

The Problem with Target-Date Funds

You may think Jane's experience is a one-time incident. After all, target-date funds are very popular. Assets in target-date funds increased each year from 2008 to 2016. They hit a record $880 billion in 2016, up from $763 billion at the end of 2015, according to Morningstar. That's a lot of money, especially when you consider that the fund category didn't even exist until the mid-2000s. It took the entire mutual-fund industry more than fifty years to reach $2 trillion in assets.

Despite this popularity, however, Jane isn't alone in her experience. In 2008, Fidelity Freedom 2010 Fund and Vanguard Target Retirement 2010 Fund—some of the biggest names in the business—both lost more than 20%. I've heard worse, though. Also in 2006, Fidelity Freedom Fund 2005—a fund targeting people *who had already retired*—lost 24%. I know the stock market plunged in 2008, but assets in a fund with a 2008 or 2010 target date should have been almost completely out of the stock market by then.

In fact, the markets hit an all-time high of fourteen thousand in October 2007, so why didn't the fund managers sell then? It seems obvious to me that a retirement fund with a target date of 2008 or 2010 should reduce its exposure to equities one to three years before the target date—especially if stocks reach an all-time high then.

In some cases, target-date funds are designed to stay significantly allocated to equities after the target retirement date, as I explain in "Understanding the Glide Path," below. But, there are other explanations for what happened in 2008.

Understanding the Glide Path

Different mutual-fund companies take different approaches when their target-date funds reach their target dates. Some companies convert the assets into a retirement-income fund (either at the target year or later); others keep the assets in the original fund and keep the same name. For example, Vanguard Target Retirement 2010 is still around, even though 2010 has long since passed.

Either way, however, what happens to the fund's asset allocation when the target date is reached depends on its glide path. A glide path is simply the shift in a target-date fund's asset allocation over time.

There are two different approaches to glide paths. A two-retirement approach reduces the fund's equity exposure over time, reaching its most conservative point *at* the target date. A through-retirement approach also reduces the fund's equity exposure over time, but does so *through* the target date, so the fund reaches its most conservative point years after the target date.

According to a recent research paper published by Morningstar, one of the key differences between target-date funds with two-retirement glide paths and target-date funds with through-retirement glide paths is the speed with which the allocation to stocks decreases. The average fund with a two-retirement glide path reaches its target retirement year with a 33% allocation to equities. Meanwhile, the average fund with a through-retirement glide path reaches its target retirement year with a 49% allocation to equities, and then lowers its equity exposure over the next twenty to thirty years before reaching a final equity allocation of 28%.

The reason? Funds with through-retirement glide paths are designed to provide greater protection against longevity risk (since stocks tend to outperform other asset classes over time).

The problem? You could end up a few years into retirement with a significant allocation to equities.

Another explanation for what happened in 2008 that's bandied about is greed: holding more assets in stocks means more profit for the companies that manage target-date funds, because actively managed stock funds generally charge higher expenses than bond funds.

Or, consider this as yet another explanation for what happened in 2008: the fund managers just didn't have the control you would expect them to have. That's because many target-date funds are simply comprised of other funds in the same fund family. For example, a Fidelity target-date fund invests in other Fidelity funds, just like a Vanguard target-date invests in other Vanguard funds. Want proof? According to Morningstar, the Vanguard target retirement 2015 fund has 99.99% of its client's money in *other* Vanguard funds as of April 30, 2017. Vanguard funds holding Vanguard funds, and Fidelity funds holding Fidelity funds, creates a possible conflict of interest.

Now, I'm not opposed to investing in funds of funds. In fact, the fund I manage does just that. However, there are two distinct differences between what I do and what large fund companies such as Vanguard and Fidelity do. First, I use mutual funds with which I have no business affiliation, meaning there is no conflict of interest. I select a fund strictly on the basis of my research strongly indicating that it is best for my shareholders. Second, I disclose the internal fees of the funds I buy, called the internal holdings fee. Target-date funds aren't required to do that. So I have exposed a built-in conflict of interest and a layer of undisclosed fees built into target-date funds.

Target-date fund managers, not managing the underlying assets of their funds themselves, may not keep on top of the overall asset allocation.

Here's the proof. According to the Fidelity Freedom Fund 2005 prospectus dated May 30, 2009, the fund's principal investing strategy is "investing in a combination of underlying Fidelity equity, fixed-income, and short-term funds using a moderate asset-allocation strategy designed for investors expected to have retired around the year 2005."

The fund, the prospectus said, works by "allocating assets among underlying Fidelity Funds according to an asset-allocation strategy that becomes increasingly conservative until it reaches 20% in domestic equity funds, 35% in investment-grade fixed-income funds, 5% in high-yield fixed-income funds, and 40% in short-term funds (approximately 10 to 15 years after the year 2005)."

But, according to Value Line Mutual Fund Analysis, Fidelity Freedom Fund 2005 had almost 40% in equities as of June 30, 2009. That's twice the amount suggested by the prospectus, a full four and a half years after the retirement date. The fund also had almost 8% of its assets invested in international equities, including the emerging markets. Looking through the prospectus, I couldn't find anything that explained how international equities could make up 8% of the fund.

You might think that mutual-fund companies changed after the debacle that was 2008. No to that, too. According to Brightscope, a company that ranks 401(k) plans, from 2007 to 2010, the targeted percentage of stocks in target-date funds rose after the financial crisis, from an average of 40% in 2007 to 43% in 2010. "Many fund companies failed to learn from the 2008 debacle, which failure will surely hurt participants again," Brightscope concluded.

Five years after I first wrote about this, in a speech made at the American Retirement Initiative's winter 2015 summit, Securities and Exchange Commission (SEC) Commissioner Luis A. Aguilar expressed similar concerns with target-date funds. "Not only have target date fund assets quadrupled since 2008, but their percentage of allocations to equities has also grown," he said. "Since 2005, many target-date funds have boosted their allocations to equities, both by extending their glide paths beyond the target date and by increasing equity allocations across the entire glide path. In and of itself, this may not be inappropriate, as the greater exposure to equities may allow for greater returns. The issue, however, is whether investors appreciate the risks involved in having a greater allocation to equities, which generally are presumed riskier than fixed-income investments."

Who's the Biggest Offender?

According to Morningstar, some target-date fund providers have stable ratios of stocks to conservative investments over time, while others (notably Fidelity, the market leader) have more fluctuations.

Separate research by Morningstar in 2013 found that thirteen of Fidelity's fourteen target-date funds performed worse than three-fourths of their competitors.

Also in 2013, the Center for Due Diligence, an independent information and strategic services firm serving retirement plan advisors, posted an analysis of Fidelity's target-date funds compared to similar offerings from the company's major competitors. When it came to funds with target retirement dates from 2010 to 2055, 79% of the Fidelity Freedom funds, 74% of the Fidelity Freedom K funds, and 68% of the Fidelity Advisor Freedom funds landed in the bottom half of category rankings.

Of course, stronger returns aren't everything. Phil Chiricotti, president of the Center for Due Diligence, said that Fidelity's more conservative glide path is one of the primary reasons its funds were underperforming, and a conservative glide path may be a good thing for risk-averse investors. But, anecdotal evidence doesn't support that, as I've explained with my discussion of what happened to some Fidelity target-date funds in 2008.

Well, you might say, that's just a problem with Fidelity. Other mutual-fund companies might do a better job. Nope—because there just aren't that many other mutual-fund companies heavily into the target-date fund business. According to an April 2013 report by the SEC's investor advisory committee, there is a high degree of saver concentration among just a few target-date funds. According to Morningstar, in 2016 three firms collectively held 71% of the market share in target-date funds: Vanguard (31.8% of market share), Fidelity (21.9%), and T. Rowe Price (16.8%). Seven firms held 88.3%. As a result, large numbers of investors, including individuals approaching retirement at the same time, will be affected by the approaches these companies adopt.

I Saw This Coming

I discussed the problem with target-date funds years ago, in the February 2010 *Navigator Newsletter*, writing, "Do the funds live up to the hype? Let's see. To me the biggest attraction these funds would have is if they did indeed proactively reallocate the portfolio to reduce the risk as you got within 10 years of retirement and eliminated nearly all of it by five years out."

Target-date funds didn't do that then, and they don't do it now.

The unfortunate thing is these funds are designed to appeal to investors such as Jane who just don't know any better. They're packaged as a turnkey approach to retirement, or, as Fidelity describes its Fidelity Freedom Funds, they're "all-in-one investment strategies that can help take the guesswork out of building and maintaining an age-based retirement portfolio." In other words, "It's easy! Just pick a fund with a date that matches your projected retirement, and we'll take care of the rest!" Sadly, many of these funds don't take care of the rest, and investors don't know it.

According to the aforementioned April 2013 SEC report, "Evidence suggests that individual investors are ill-equipped to identify those risk disparities among similar seeming funds. For example, on a survey commissioned by the SEC, only 36% of respondents (including 48% of target-date fund owners and 26% of non-owners) correctly answered a true-false question regarding whether target date funds provide guaranteed income after retirement. Thirty percent (including 25% of owners and 34% of non-owners) answered incorrectly that target-date funds do provide guaranteed income. Fifteen percent of respondents said whether there is a guarantee depends on the fund and 20% said they didn't know."

Moreover, investors can't even rely on the professionals to help them with target-date funds, because the professionals don't understand them either. According to the aforementioned April 2013 SEC report, many professional pension fund consultants—those are the people who help select retirement plan fund options—underestimate the risk of target-date funds.

One unpublished study, conducted for PIMCO in 2010, found that, although the average target-date fund exposed investors nearing retirement to a significantly higher maximum potential loss than most consultants surveyed deemed appropriate, only about 35% of those consultants viewed the glide paths as somewhat too highly inappropriate (i.e., too aggressive). "In other words, almost two-thirds of these pension consultants assumed that funds were invested more conservatively than was in fact the case," says the report.

"Bonds are Terrible"—Warren Buffett, May 8, 2017

Now, here's the really bad news about target-date funds (as if what I've written isn't bad enough): today's macroeconomic conditions are making the problem even worse.

Even if target-date funds work exactly as they're supposed to work—which I've already shown they don't—there's a problem given their heavy allocation to bonds.

What, you may ask? Aren't bonds supposed to be safer than stocks? In theory, yes; more bonds should make a fund safer, because bonds tend to be less risky than stocks.

But that's not always the case. Don't take my word for it; consider the words of America's great stock market investor, Warren Buffett, who has made billions of dollars knowing where to invest his and his client's money, thanks in part to his uncanny ability to recognize trends *before* the masses do. In a televised interview on May

8, 2017, Buffett said, "Bonds are a terrible choice against stocks and it's dictated by the mathematics. Thirty-year Treasury bonds are 3% now, while stocks now trade for an average of about 18 times forward earnings. Stocks offer growth while bonds offer fixed interest rates. Stocks are dirt cheap."

Right now, however, the bond market is near an all-time high, as gauged by the low yield of the ten-year US Treasury. (Remember, bond prices and bond yields are inversely correlated. As the price goes up, the yield goes down.)

The first problem with the bond market today is that in moving assets from stocks to bonds as the retirement date approaches, a fund manager is forced to sell stocks and buy bonds, and those bonds are, simply explained, expensive. So by buying bonds at today's level, a portfolio manager is actually adding risk to a fund instead of reducing it, as you would expect in a target-date fund.

Additionally, should interest rates revert to their historic norms (which they will, because they always have), bond prices will fall. The historic norm of the ten-year US Treasury yield is roughly 4% compared to 1.3759%, its all-time low reached in July 2016. And, the increase in a bond's yield is always proportional to the decrease in a bond's price. If a ten-year bond yield increases by 1%, there would be a 5% drop in its price. So when the bond market normalizes, there could be a 10% to 15% drop in bond prices. This drop may be a fatal blow to retirees who've been thinking that as time marches on, their target-date funds will take on less risk.

These misunderstandings may be a ticking time bomb for the next generation of American retirees. T. Rowe Price, for example, uses a 90% stock and 10% bond allocation for investors thirty years from retirement, but a 20% stock and 80% bond mix thirty years after the retirement date. That's a lot of bonds!

Again, five years after I first wrote about this, in his speech made at the American Retirement Initiative's winter 2015 summit, Aguilar expressed similar concerns with target-date funds. "The belief is that an improving economy will eventually force the Federal Reserve to raise interest rates, and that this may cause another 'taper tantrum,' in which bond prices plummet," he said, adding that this possibility raises a number of questions for target-date fund providers.

- How do we warn investors about this potential market disruption?
- What are these funds doing to prepare for another possible taper tantrum? Are they diversifying into other assets besides bonds?
- If so, does this present new risks that should be disclosed to investors?

These are all good questions, if I do say so myself (as I have).

The Dawdling SEC

The good news, if there is any, is that the SEC got wind of this problem, and 2010 proposed a rule that, if adopted, would require any target-date fund that includes the target date in its name to disclose its allocation at the projected retirement date "immediately adjacent to" the first use of the fund's name in marketing materials. The rule would also require more disclosure about a fund's asset allocation and glide path. The SEC invited comments from the public, but for whatever reason, nothing came of this review in 2010.

Then, in 2013, the SEC's investor advisory committee adopted recommendations asking the agency to rewrite its proposed rule on target-date retirement funds. The recommendations would expand the 2010 SEC proposal with five recommendations. Mutual fund companies, the committee said, should

- develop a glide path illustration for target-date funds based on risk rather than asset allocation alone;
- adopt a standard methodology to be used in the risk-based and asset-allocation glide path illustrations;
- clearly explain the assumptions used to design and manage the fund to attain the target risk level over the life of the fund;

- warn that target-date fund returns are not guaranteed and that losses are possible, including at or after the target date; and
- amend fee disclosure requirements to show the impact of those costs over the lifetime of the investment.

"In making this change in disclosure, we are actually going to teach investors something really important that most of them don't understand," said James Glassman, a committee member and founding executive director of the George W. Bush Institute, at a hearing. "There is more to risk than asset allocation."

I thought that was a good sign that something—finally!—would be done about target-date funds. Investors needed to be informed that these funds have better marketing strategies than investment strategies.

I was even more hopeful when, in 2014, the SEC reopened its 2010 proposed rule for public comment in 2014.

But guess what? We're still waiting for a final rule.

And if you think government always works that slowly, consider this. In the spring of 2013, it took the SEC only weeks to declare that public companies could announce vital information via social media. Let's hope that they move as fast on a matter that affects most Americans' 401(k) accounts.

Change on the Horizon?

That said, in his speech at the American Retirement Initiative's winter 2015 summit, Aguilar did express concerns with target-date funds.

"These funds are particularly attractive to investors who are not financially experienced," he said. "Evidence suggests that investors may perceive these funds to be virtually risk-free…Target date funds, however, do not contain guarantees. Investors in these funds are not assured they will have sufficient retirement income at the target date, and there is no guarantee that investors will not lose some, or even all, of their investment."

According to Aguilar, the experience of target-date fund investors during the financial crisis should have been a wake-up call that these funds were not performing as advertised; he criticized the fact that no rules about disclosures have been passed since then. He points out that the need for the SEC to act "has taken on an added urgency in recent years, as investors have continued to invest in target-date funds in record numbers."

"The SEC staff should move quickly to advise the Commission on how best to move forward to help individual investors and plan providers," he said. "It is imperative that investors better understand the risks presented by target-date funds."

Aguilar also suggested that the SEC dust off its 2010 target-date fund proposal and consider what actions may be appropriate, in light of all the evidence gathered.

"The consequences of investors continuing to be ill-informed about the inherent risks of target-date funds are simply too grave," he said.

Not Alpha, but Ow-pha!

You've heard of alpha, but do you know what it means?

Alpha is an investment term that refers to how your investment has performed in relation to the amount of risk it is taking.

For example, if your investment has an alpha of zero, it is considered to be neutral regarding its risk-return ratio. Simply put, it did exactly what you would expect.

An investment with a positive alpha, on the other hand, returned more than expected. If your investment's alpha is 1.25, it returned 25% more than expected based on the level of risk it is exposed to.

A negative alpha, meanwhile, indicates that your investment underperformed its expectations.

Good money managers always seeking to provide their shareholders with positive alpha. If a fund has a positive alpha, the manager did a very good job, even if a fund lost money. That's because investments should be measured in relative terms—relative to how they are expected to do. (That's also why we compare investments to benchmarks, but that's another story.)

"Ow-pha" is a term I coined with the help of my business partner Joseph Visconti. It describes how investors in target-date retirement funds feel when they realize they were duped by fancy marketing. It's not just "ow!" It's "ow-pha!"

Picture this. You invest your savings in hypothetical target retirement 2020 fund many years ago because you were told the fund was designed to follow your path as you aged. It would slowly and surely reduce your risk as you inched closer to that hammock on the beach.

You were really glad to hear that in 2018 when the market had its first 20% decline in more than decade. You didn't have to worry, you thought, because your 2020 fund had surely by then reduced its risk to a level where you would only experience a small dip. There is no way a 2020 fund would participate in the full market decline, right?

Wrong!

Three of the largest 2020 target-date funds all lost more than the market in 2018. That's the moment when investors say "ow-pha!" instead of "alpha."

I've explained what's wrong with target-date funds; now I'd like to show you some examples focusing on these three 2020 target-date funds, which, as noted, are designed for individuals retiring in or very close to the year 2020.

Many such funds simply aren't living up to expectations and are failing to protect the soon-to-be retirees who invest in them from big market losses. If anything it should be clear from this chapter, it's that target-date funds can't protected you from losses. They didn't in 2008, they didn't in 2018, and they won't in the future.

Fidelity Freedom 2020 Fund (FFFDX)

Designed for investors who anticipate retiring in or within a few years of the fund's target retirement year, this fund "seeks high total return until its target retirement date. Thereafter, the fund's seeks high current income first and capital appreciation second.

The fund seeks to achieve this goal by allocating assets among underlying Fidelity funds according to a "neutral" asset-allocation strategy that adjusts over time until it reaches an allocation similar to that of the Freedom Income Fund.

Where does the fund stand now, a year before its target date? As of 12/31/18, the fund's composition was 35.26% domestic equities, 20.06% international equities, 36.14% bonds, and 8.54% short-term debt (such as money market funds and US Treasuries).

In theory, that might seem reasonable. You need equities for growth as you approach retirement. And the fund has delivered growth over the longer term. As of 12/31/18, its ten-year average annual return was a solid 8.42%.

But you want to cut your risk exposure back as you near retirement to minimize the effects of market volatility. You can tolerate such swings when you have years to ride them out, but when you need to withdraw your money, those swings become problematic. Is FFFDX's 55% total equity allocation reasonable a year before your retirement date?

In 2018, FFFDX was down 5.20%, more than the S&P 500 Index (down 4.38%), the Fidelity Freedom 2020 Composite Index (down 3.75%), and the Morningstar Target-Date 2020 category (down 4.49%), all of which it shows as benchmarks. So not only was FFFDX losing money for retirees invested in it a year before needed that money; it was losing money faster than all of its benchmarks, even one operated by Fidelity itself! Ow-pha!

Now skeptics might note that FFFDX has only been down in three of the past ten calendar years. I understand that point. But to be down so much a year before the target date tells me something is wrong.

It's also worth noting that FFFDX has $26.2 billion in assets as of the end of 2018. That's a lot of shareholder accounts.

Vanguard Target Retirement 2020 Fund (VTWNX)

Like FFFDX, VTWNX has considerable assets under management: $31.7 billion.

Also designed for investors who anticipate retiring in or within a few years of the fund's target retirement year (2018 to 2022, according to Vanguard), VTWNX invests in five Vanguard index funds, holding approximately 55% of assets in stocks and 45% in bonds.

Its objective is to provide broad diversification while incrementally decreasing exposure to stocks and increasing exposure to bonds as each fund's target retirement date approaches. It continues to adjust for approximately seven years after its target date until its allocations match that of the Target Retirement Income Fund. So in 2027, it should be a bond fund.

That's a more aggressive transition to bonds than FFFDX offered. But where does the fund stand now a year before its target date? As of 12/31/18, the fund's composition was 53.18% equities (international and domestic combined) and 46.82% bonds. So about the same as FFFDX.

Not surprisingly, the fund lost money in 2018, just as FFFDX did. In 2018, VTWNX was down 4.24%, more than the S&P 500 Index (again, down 4.38%) and its benchmark Target Retirement 2020 Composite Index (down 4.13%). Ow-pha!

Interesting for a fund that shows its risk potential being a three on a scale of one to five. If you're preparing to retire and have amassed, say, a $1,000,000 portfolio, how do you feel about your nest egg being down more than $40,000 this year?

T. Rowe Price Retirement 2020 Fund (TRRBX)

Let's look at one more example, TRRBX, which, like other target-date funds, invests in a diversified portfolio of other T. Rowe Price stock and bond funds. It has $18.4 billion in assets under management.

T. Rowe Price offers more detail on its website than many other mutual fund marketers, indicating that as the fund nears its target retirement date, its allocation between T. Rowe Price stock and bond funds will become more conservative based on a pre-determined glide path.

But the website notes that "the allocations shown in the glide path are referred to as 'neutral' allocations because they do not reflect the tactical decisions made by T. Rowe Price to overweight or underweight a particular asset class or sector based on its market outlook."

T. Rowe Price makes its holding harder to find than the other funds I've mentioned. It says 97.8% of its assets are allocated to "other" as of 11/30/18. (How's that for transparency?) Digging a little deeper and looking at its top 10 holdings, though, six are stock funds.

But that shouldn't matter, since TRRBX's managers can reallocate based on what portfolio managers think is best given current market conditions, right? That means the fund should have performed better than other target-date funds that struggled in 2018? Because surely its managers reallocated as the market took a dive?

Nope. As of 12/31/18, the fund's handy risk-potential chart shows its risk as somewhere between "moderate" and "higher," meaning portfolio managers haven't reallocated. In 2018, the fund was down 4.94%, more than its benchmarks: the S&P Target Date 2020 Index (down 4.16%) and the Lipper Mixed-Asset Target 2020 Funds Average (down 4.59%). Ow-pha!

The Return of the Bear

What happened in 2018? Santa left a lump of coal in most investors' stockings in 2018. The market shuddered, and it was bad. On December 24, the S&P 500 Index fell into bear-market territory (a loss of 20% from its high) in post-market trading.

That was the worst Christmas Eve trading session ever, and the first time the index had entered a bear market since 2009. And it happened quickly: In just ten calendar days, the index fell about 250 points, close to 10%.

The S&P 500 Index wasn't alone. Other indices—the Nasdaq Composite Index and Russell 2000 Index—had already entered bear markets.

This provided a harsh reminder to target-date-fund investors that broad diversification doesn't ensure they won't experience difficult losses—and perhaps harkened back to 2008 when target-date investors on the verge of retirement experienced hefty losses.

Callout: "Imagine being two years away from retirement and seeing your 401(k)—which you may have thought was shielded from massive market corrections—tank by more than 20%. That was the reality in 2008 for workers who had invested their savings in target-date funds" (CNBC, September 2018).

Learning from the Past

When you're a target-date investor and market volatility gets you and your portfolio down, you're in a tough spot. Some target-date investors have many years to make up ground before they retire and start withdrawing assets, but many others hope to retire soon. They have only two choices: work longer to make up the losses or simply learn to live with less in retirement. Neither is likely appealing.

But that's what happened in 2008. Target-date funds with retirement dates beyond 2020 experienced losses exceeding 30%. But investors in those funds had years to continue saving, and they were able to take advantage of the bull market that started in March 2009. Investors in nearer-dated funds, including those set to retire in 2010, weren't so fortunate.

Consider those unlucky enough to be allocated to the Oppenheimer Transition 2010 Fund, which had around 70% of its assets allocated to equities just two years before it reached its target date, according to Morningstar. It experienced a 41% loss in 2008. Investors just couldn't recover from that. How could you?

And 2008 unearthed another risk: fixed income. Widely considered a safe haven, it turned out bonds weren't what they appeared to be, either. Some target-date funds had aggressively allocated their fixed-income component to risky high-yield bond funds, which can move in the same direction as equities.

Did portfolio managers learn from the past?

No, but don't take my word for it. "What managers generally have not done is reduce their overall equity exposure," says a September 2018 CNBC article, "These 401(k) Funds Took a Beating In 2008—And It Could Happen Again." "If anything, they've added more stock exposure for investors who are in the middle of their careers."

"This way, these savers can continue to capture market gains and stave off the risk they will outlive their savings in retirement," said Jeff Holt, director, multiasset and alternative strategies at Morningstar, quoted in the CNBC article. "Target-date funds aren't fundamentally different in how they are built now versus 2008. They still hold a significant amount of equities at the retirement date."

If anything, 2018 made the point that target-date funds haven't changed loud and clear. Before December 2018, we'd been in the midst of a historically significant bull market since the last bear market ended in March 2009. That's almost ten-year of bull market, which is virtually unprecedented. Anyone with any sense knew we would undoubtedly experience a market correction at some point—but target-date fund managers didn't seem to care. They just rode the highs, basking in the glow of positive performance—until they couldn't.

Callout: "It's a lot of money to have sitting around in target-date funds—and the 5% of it lost by portfolio managers in 2018 is close to $4 billion" (Mark Anthony Grimaldi, January 2019).

As I noted, the assets under management of the three funds I reviewed are notable: FFFDX has $26.2 billion, VTWNX has $31.7 billion, and TRRBX has $18.4 billion. That's a total of $76.3 billion in shareholder accounts.

How much is $76.3 billion? Well, is you had it, you could give ever man, woman, and child in the United States $234. You could give every retiree in the United States (an estimated population of around 50 million) $1,526. Or you could be selfish and keep it to yourself, in which case you'd have to spend $4,180,822 a day for the next fifty years to deplete your stash (and that's assuming you stuff it under your mattress, without any interest compounding!).

The point is, it's a lot of money to have sitting around in target-date funds—and the 5% of it lost by portfolio managers in 2018 is close to $4 billion. That's even more money to lose on behalf of trusting retirees. Ow-pha!

CALLOUT: "The only time people really learn when it comes to investments is if they lose a lot of money. You never learn anything from making money; you learn it all on the downside" (Aaron Pottichen, senior vice president at Alliant Retirement Consulting, quoted by CNBC, September 2018).

What Can You Do?

We've established that target-date funds are riskier investments than they're widely considered, and that the SEC isn't acting promptly to correct those misperceptions. That being the case, what can you do?

It's simple: Don't invest in target-date funds. Ever.

It just doesn't make sense. Putting everyone of the same age into the same asset allocation defeats the purpose of financial planning, which is supposed to construct a portfolio appropriate to an individual investor's investment goals and risk tolerance, and change it over time based on changes in that an individual investor's circumstances. Target-date funds are like a doctor writing every fifty-year-old a prescription for blood pressure medication, because that's what all fifty-year-olds need, and then switching the prescription to cholesterol-lowering medication in five years, because that's what all fifty-five-year-olds need.

Remember Jane, whose target-date retirement fund lost 20.67% just two years before its maturity date? She gets it. "I've always been told if something seems too good to be true, it probably is, and these funds were that," she says. "Somebody was sleeping at the wheel, and I hope what you're writing helps avoid another person making the same mistake that I did. People have to understand that these funds have disappointed in the past, and will most likely disappoint in the future."

So there you have it. I showed you that inside your 401(k) lies another set of lies designed to keep you from achieving a retirement free from income tax and true investment diversification.

Chapter X
It's Ok I Got This...

Getting the Government Out of Your Retirement Plan

There's no way around it. The government is getting involved in your retirement. A number of states are now forcing small businesses to create retirement plans for private-sector employees, and under the fiduciary rule, financial advisors who work with retirement plans are subject to a much higher level of accountability. These may sound like good things, but they have significant negative implications. The more the government is involved in the retirement savings, the greater your tax bill will be.

The Great American Retirement Crisis

Why does the government care so much about your retirement? Older Americans are facing a financial crisis. According to the Employee Benefit Research Institute, around a third of US workers wonder whether they'll be able to cover basic living costs when they retire. One reason, says CNBC, is that about fifty-five million US workers don't have access to an employer-based retirement savings plan. Sure, those people could open an individual retirement account (IRA) with an investment company, assuming they qualify, but they haven't. Only one in three American households has an IRA, according to the Investment Company Institute. The government wants to save these people from inevitable doom.

Enter Your Benevolent Government

This increase in the number of Americans struggling to save for retirement has led a number of state governments to take action. As of this writing, nine states—California, Connecticut, Illinois, Maryland, Massachusetts, New Jersey, New York, Oregon, and Washington—have either implemented or planned to implement legislation that will create retirement plans for private-sector employees who don't have access to an employer-sponsored retirement plan.

Generally, this legislation forces small businesses of a certain size to set up retirement plans (usually Roth IRAs) using investment firms and low-risk funds chosen by the state. The laws require the small businesses who are affected to set aside a percentage of every worker's salary each month for the retirement fund (although workers could opt out of contributing).

This may sound like a good idea, but as the proverb goes, "The road to hell is paved with good intentions." First, it will put an undue burden on small companies, many of which are already struggling to keep costs down. Second, it will force most retirement-plan participants into target-date retirement funds, which are problematic, as I explained previously. It will also expose individuals to the 401(k) trap, by which I mean the fact that your 401(k) plan will likely be the most taxed of all your assets.

And, it will increase the size and reach of the government, which is rarely, if ever, a good thing.

More Meddling: The Fiduciary Rule and 401(k) Plan Advice

As I mentioned, the government is getting involved in your retirement with the fiduciary rule, under which financial advisors who work with retirement plans are subject to a much higher level of accountability. While this may make sense, especially after so many retirees lost their assets in the global financial crisis, it actually has some poorly understood implications. Specifically, if the fiduciary rule is not implemented, 401(k) plan holders will continue to receive no professional advice, and if it is implemented, 401(k) plan holders will have to pay high fees. In other words, the fiduciary rule is a lose-lose. But let's start at the beginning.

What Is the Fiduciary Rule?

The fiduciary rule is a piece of legislation that expands the definition of "investment advice fiduciary" under the Employee Retirement Income Security Act of 1974 (ERISA).

At its core, this vast piece of legislation—which is 1,023 pages long—elevates all financial professionals who work with retirement plans or provide retirement planning advice to the level of a "fiduciary."

A fiduciary is simply a person or organization that is legally and ethically bound to act in the best interests of the person or organization. That is a seemingly innocuous mandate, but it's thrown the financial industry into turmoil.

History of the Fiduciary Rule

Historically, the Department of Labor (DOL) has regulated financial advice surrounding retirement under the Employee Retirement Income Security Act (ERISA).

But ERISA is an old law. It was enacted in 1974, and has not been updated to reflect changes in retirement savings trends, particularly the shift from defined-benefit plans (such as pensions) to defined-contribution plans (such as 401(k)s) and the massive growth in individual retirement accounts [IRAs]).

So the DOL proposed some reforms in 2010. That went nowhere, thanks to fierce protests from the financial industry regarding the costs of implementation.

Then, in 2015, President Obama proposed an overhaul to the rules, stating, "It's a very simple principle: you want to give financial advice, you've got to put your client's interests first."

The final version of what we know as the fiduciary rule was issued in April 2016, and was scheduled to be phased in from April 10, 2017, through January 1, 2018.

Delay after delay had occurred, however.

In June 2016, eight industry and trade groups filed a lawsuit against the DOL, claiming that the DOL didn't have the authority to enact the new rules.

Then, in February 2017, President Donald Trump ordered the DOL to review the fiduciary rule, considering whether it is likely to harm investors due to a reduction in savings offerings, whether it has resulted in disruptions within the retirement services industry that may adversely affect investors or retirees, and whether it is likely to cause an increase in litigation and prices for retirement services. If the answer was yes to any of these points, or if the DOL found the rule to be inconsistent with President Trump's stated priority "to empower Americans to make their own financial decisions," they were instructed to rescind or revise the fiduciary rule.

In March 2017, the DOL called for a sixty-day delay to the fiduciary rule's April 10, 2017, implementation and to open up comments on the issues raised in the Trump memo.

This created a lot of confusion, leading two of the world's two largest asset managers—Vanguard and BlackRock—to call for a more significant delay.

But the time may have come for the fiduciary rule to be implemented. The fiduciary rule officially went into effect in June 2017, but enforcement was placed on hold until January 1, 2018. Now, the rule is supposed to be phased in by July 1, 2019.

What Does the Fiduciary Rule Mean?

Under the fiduciary rule, financial advisors who work with retirement plans are subject to a much higher level of accountability.

First, what does the DOL consider a retirement plan? First, the new rule covers defined-contribution plans: 401(k) plans, 403(b) plans, employee stock ownership plans, Simplified Employee Pension (SEP) plans, and savings incentive match (SIMPLE) plans. Second, it covers defined-benefit plans, such as pension plans that promise a certain payment to the participant. Finally, it covers IRAs.

Taxable accounts—those funded with after-tax dollars—are not considered retirement plans, even if the funds are earmarked for retirement savings.

And, financial advisors, even if giving advice regarding retirement plans, have a *little* leeway: they can provide *education*, such as general investment advice based on a person's age or income, and they aren't subject to the fiduciary rule when clients call and request a specific investment.

So any financial advisor providing advice about those retirement plans are subject to a much higher level of accountability.

Previously, they were subject to the "suitability" standard, which meant that as long as an investment recommendation met a client's objective, it was considered appropriate. Now, fiduciaries are subject to the "fiduciary" standard. That means financial professionals are legally obligated to put their client's best interests first rather than simply finding "suitable" investments.

That involves a number of things. Financial advisors must clearly disclose all compensation (fees and commissions) in dollar form to clients. And financial advisors who want to accept commissions must provide clients with a disclosure agreement, called a Best Interest Contract Exemption (BICE), when there could be a conflict of interest, such as the financial advisor receiving a higher commission for selling a certain product. Financial advisors must also proactively monitor a client's circumstances investments over time.

An Example: Ms. Suitability

To illustrate the difference between these two standards, imagine that a financial advisor has a client—a middle-aged woman named Ms. Suitability—who is long-term investor and is not worried about market volatility.

Under the suitability standard, the financial advisor can meet with Ms. Suitability to determine suitable investments for her at that point in time. Given Ms. Suitability's situation, it seems reasonable that the financial advisor would invest most of her money in stock mutual funds.

Now, imagine that those stock mutual funds are operated by the entity that employs the financial advisor. The financial advisor would give Ms. Suitability a prospectus that tells her in confusing legalese that about the potential conflict of interest, and also that the financial advisor receives a perpetual trailing fee on top of his sales commission. Once Ms. Suitability leaves the financial advisor's office, he has little further legal obligation to monitor her investment.

Under the fiduciary standard, all conflicts of interest must be disclosed, so the financial advisor will have to clearly explain the relationship between the mutual funds he recommends and the entity that employs him, as well as how he is compensated. Also, because a fiduciary has a "duty to care," the financial advisor must monitor Ms. Suitability's changing financial situation and her investments to ensure they are suitable not yet when he makes them, but as long as she holds them.

<<Obama's Council of Economic Advisers estimated that non-fiduciary advice costs Americans 1 percentage point of their return annually, which amounts to $17 billion each year.>>

Pros and Cons of the Fiduciary Rule

It's easy to understand why someone would think the forty-year-old ERISA rules needed updating.

Supporters of the fiduciary rule believe it will increase transparency for investors and prevent abuses on the part of financial advisors, such as excessive commissions and investment churning for reasons of compensation.

However, the legislation has met with opposition from some financial advisors who would rather be held to a "suitability" standard than a "fiduciary" standard because the latter will cost them a lot of money, both in lost commissions and in compliance.

It would be particularly difficult for smaller, independent firms, which may not have the financial resources to invest in the technology and the compliance expertise to meet the new rule's requirements. Some firms may be forced out of business.

That's what happened in the United Kingdom after it passed similar rules in 2011. Since then, the number of financial advisors there has dropped by about 22.5%.

In fact, it's already happening here in the United States. The brokerage divisions of MetLife Inc. and American International Group were sold in anticipation of the fiduciary rule.

Some also fear the fiduciary rule, in reducing or eliminating the payment of commissions, would force financial advisors to shift fees onto individuals, pricing many lower-and middle-income investors out of the market.

One final criticism of the fiduciary rule: It doesn't matter. Financial advisors who are bad apples, say critics, will continue to be bad apples regardless of the rule.

The Fiduciary Rule and 401(k) Plan Advice

That's a lot of background information, so let's get to the crux of the issue.

If your financial advisor actually represents your 401(k) plan or has been hired by your company to manage employee plan accounts, then he or she can manage your 401(k) plan. That's because such a financial advisor (and his or her firm) is considered the "plan fiduciary." He or she must comply with ERISA laws and all the government agencies that enforce those laws.

Now, what if your financial advisor is not directly related to your 401(k) plan? Then can he or she manage your 401(k) plan? It depends.

To manage your 401(k) plan, your financial advisor must be a registered investment advisor (RIA) under the Investment Advisers Act of 1940. That requires your financial advisor to obtain certain securities licenses, and his or her firm must allow this activity and declare on their firm brochure.

Some firms allow this activity, and others do not. Independent firms and those that charge financial planning fees typically allow it; larger brokerage houses typically do not (because it is difficult to supervise on a large scale).

If your financial advisor manages your 401(k) plan, he or she will not be able to withdraw fees directly from the account; you will be invoiced for this work.

Some financial advisors will log directly into your plan and manage the account continuously, provide performance reporting. Others will provide you with recommended trades, and you must enter them yourself.

Who can't manage your 401(k) plan? Traditional stockbrokers and financial planners, who are paid commissions for their recommendations. That creates a conflict of interest.

Another Example: Ms. Suitability

Let's make that more comprehensible with another example. Say Ms. Suitability has commission-based accounts—a brokerage account and a Roth IRA—at Happy Brokerage. As the firm's name would suggest, she's happy with the service she receives.

Then she gets a letter from Happy Brokerage. It says that due to changes made in anticipation of the fiduciary rule, Ms. Suitability has two choices.

First, she can keep her existing commission-based accounts as they are, but she will be unable to make any changes inside the Roth IRA going forward.

Second, she can shift her Roth into a different type of account that would require her to pay a yearly fee and have a financial advisor actively manage her retirement assets. The annual fee would be 1% of assets. That fee is intended to pay Ms. Suitability's financial advisor for the time he spends managing investments in the account (which commissions previously did), but Ms. Suitability doesn't want to pay a 1% fee, because the investments in her account rarely change. This isn't a hypothetical example, either. It's already happened to many investors—investors just like you.

Pulling It All Together

Okay, so what does this all mean?

If the fiduciary rule is not implemented, things will go on as they have, and individuals without RIAs—most investors—will continue to manage their own retirement plans. They will use discount brokerages, select their own investments, or perhaps use one of the new robo-advisors (computer algorithms that invest for you based on factors such as age and risk appetite).

If the fiduciary rule is implemented, the big players in the 401(k) industry—firms like Vanguard, Fidelity, and Principle—will begin pushing clients such as Ms. Suitability into fee-based accounts.

In fact, they've already begun doing so, because it's good for business. While financial advisory firms' revenues have remained essentially flat since 2014, revenue from fee accounts has grown by more than 5%, according to research from Aite Group. And among the biggest firms—Merrill Lynch, Morgan Stanley, Wells Fargo, and UBS—fee-based investments now make up 38% of assets managed.

That could be costly. If your financial advisor charges an annual management of 1%, which is fairly average, and you have $500,000 in retirement savings, you would pay $5,000 in fees every year.

So 401(k) plan holders will either continue to receive no professional advice, or will have to pay high fees. Both are bad.

The Solution: No More Meddling!

Okay, that's not going to happen. But, given the problems with state-mandated retirement plans for small businesses and the fiduciary rule, what can a small business or investor do to safeguard its, his, or her retirement?

To preface my answer, do you remember the 1983 movie *WarGames?* In case it's before your time, it's a 1983 American Cold War science-fiction film. The film follows a young hacker who accesses the War Operation Plan Response (WOPR), a US military supercomputer programmed to predict possible outcomes of nuclear war. Believing that the WOPR is a computer game, the hacker gets it to run a nuclear war simulation. But the WOPR believes the game is real, links to the country's nuclear weapons control system, and attempts to start World War III. At the end of the movie, the WOPR realizes that the only winning move is *not playing*.

The same applies here. Investors should steer their retirement savings away from any and all government involvement. Every time the government gets involved in your retirement, it will cost you—either in more fees or more taxes or both.

Why Companies Don't Offer 401(k) Plans?

Working for a small business has many benefits, but retirement plans generally aren't one of them. Just a quarter of firms with fewer than fifty employees have defined-contribution plans (that include 401(k) plans) in place, according to a 2014 study by Capital One. Why? Because they're costly to set up and maintain.

First, there are initial setup fees. Then there are annual maintenance fees. Other fees you might incur include record-keeping fees, investment management, consulting or advisory fees, revenue-sharing fees, rollover fees, and discrimination testing, which ensure that your plan is properly balanced between employees and managers. If you're a new plan, you may also have to pay for an annual, legally required ERISA bond. (ERISA, the Employee Retirement Income Security Act, sets rules for private sector-employee benefit plans. An ERISA bond is simply insurance that protects your 401(k) plan against losses that are caused by fraud.)

In addition, there are many different 401(k) plans with an assortment of complex fee structures. Fees are generally handled in one of four ways. Asset-based fees are paid based on the amount of assets in the plan (typically around 2.5% of assets). Per-person fees are paid based either on how many eligible employees you have or the number or actual plan participants (from around $10 per month to more than $750 per month per person). Transaction-based fees are paid based on the execution of a particular service. And then there are flat-rate fees, which are fixed charges. Many plans charge fees based on a combination of these categories—for example, a high per-participant fee combined with a lower flat rate). These costs can be charged as one-time fees or an ongoing fees.

Moreover, some employers that sponsor 401(k) plans pay for all associated costs, including investment fees and costs. Some pay for little, with any expenses paid out of the plan's assets (meaning, fees are passed on to plan participants). Sometimes costs are shared by plan sponsors (the employer) and participants (employees).

You can see then why it's hard to quantify just how costly a 401(k) plan is. It's virtually impossible to get average ranges for fees.

One thing we do know, however, is that these fees add up. Initial setup fees, for example, might run $500 to $3,000, depending on the size of your company and the types of benefits you choose. Then most businesses should plan to spend up to $10,000 more per year for maintenance, most of it on administrative fees. You might also plan on $100 to $300 per hour for investment advice and initial consulting and around $1,000 to $2,500 per year for discrimination testing.

And don't forget the soft costs. Do you have the human resources staff to handle services related to 401(k) compliance, IRS deadlines, and payroll administration? And who will help answer employee questions? You may need to hire additional staff or outsource these functions.

In sum, the paperwork to set up a 401(k) plan, as well as the costs, can be overwhelming for many small business owners, many of whom who often juggle many different responsibilities and don't have the staff to focus on benefits.

Plus, there are better options, which I'll discuss separately.

Chapter XI

I Did What??

Fact: A Smart 401(k) can tell the difference between Income and Capital gains

Earned Income and Capital Gains: The Ins and Outs of Taxation

"Our new Constitution is now established, and has an appearance that promises permanency; but in this world nothing can be said to be certain, except death and taxes," wrote Benjamin Franklin in 1789 in a letter to Jean-Baptiste Leroy. While true, Franklin could hardly have anticipated the complication of today's tax code, which is 74,608 pages long. That is 187 times longer than it was a century ago, according to Wolters Kluwer, CCH, which has taken on the less-than-exciting task of analyzing the tax code since 1913. Let's try to make the subject simple by breaking it down into two parts: ordinary income taxes and capital gains taxes. For fun, I'll also throw in some information about 401(k) plans, the (allegedly) great savior of Americans' retirement.

Ordinary People, Ordinary Income

Ordinary income is simple to define. It is the income you earn by providing services or selling goods. So it would include your wages (whether you are employed by a company or self-employed), bonuses, commissions, interest, rent, royalties, and the like. For a business, it would include profits earned from selling goods or services. Let's look at two examples, one for a private individual and one for a business.

Individual: Let's say you earn $50,000 per year working for a major retailer. If you have no other source of income, you will report $50,000 of gross income on your year-end tax return. If you also receive $2,000 in rental income from a property you lease, you would report an additional $24,000 a year in gross income, for a total of $74,000.

Business: Let's say you sell $200,000 worth of goods in a year, but your total operating expenses are $125,000. You would report the difference, $75,000, as a profit.

How Ordinary Income Is Taxed

Ordinary income is taxed at different rates. It depends on the amount of income received from a given taxpayer in a given tax year. Single filers pay different rates than married filers, for example. And those who earn more pay a higher percentage of their income.

Tax rates range from 10% to 39.6%, but calculating them is not as simple as multiplying your income by a given tax rate. That's because tax rates are so-called marginal rates. For example, if you earn $10,000 in 2018, $9,525 would be taxed at the 10% tax rate (so you would owe $952.50 on it), and the remaining $675 would be taxed at the 15% tax rate (so you would owe $101.25 on it). That's a total of $1,053.75, making your actual tax rate 10.54%. Sound complicated? The folks at the Tax Foundation were kind enough to simplify it for us, as the tables below illustrate.

Note that your personal income tax can also be offset with deductions. They essentially reduce your income for tax purposes. The result is what is called your adjusted income. You can take a standard deduction—in 2018, it is $6,500 if you file as a single person, $13,000 if you and your spouse file jointly, and $9,550 if you file as head of household. You can also itemize your deductions if you think they will add up to more than the standard deduction.

Married Tax Brackets

Marginal Rate	Income Range	Taxes You Pay
10%	$0 to $19,050	10% of taxable income
12%	$19,051 to $77,400	$1,905 plus 12% of the income over $19,050
22%	$77,401 to $165,000	$8,907 plus 22% of the income over $77,400
24%	$165,001 to $315,000	$28,179 plus 24% of the income over $165,000
32%	$315,001 to $400,000	$64,178 plus 32% of the income over $315,000
35%	$400,001 to $600,000	$91,378 plus 35% of the income over $400,000
37%	Over $600,000	$161,378 plus 37% of the income over $600,000

Single Tax Brackets

Marginal Rate	Income Range	Taxes You Pay
10%	$0 to $9,525	10% of taxable income
12%	$9,526 to $38,790	$953 plus 12% of the income over $9,525
22%	$38,791 to $82,500	$4,464 plus 22% of the income over $38,790

24%	$82,501 to $157,500	$14,080 plus 24% of the income over $82,500
32%	$157,501 to $200,000	$32,080 plus 32% of the income over $157,500
35%	$200,001 to $500,000	$45,680 plus 35% of the income over $200,000
37%	Over $500,000	$150,679 plus 37% of the income over $500,000

Beware the AMT!

Then there is the dreaded alternative minimum tax (AMT). The AMT is a parallel tax system that requires high-income taxpayers to calculate their tax bill twice—once under the ordinary income tax system, then again under the AMT. The taxpayer then pays the higher of the two. This controversial system was created in the 1960s to prevent high-income taxpayers from avoiding taxes. But AMT is a complication best left to professionals.

Reducing Ordinary Income with a 401(k) Plan—A Fool's Errand

Now that we know what ordinary income is and how it is taxed, let's add the 401(k) plan into our discussion. Can't income tax be reduced by contributing to a 401(k) plan?

A 401(k) plan is a retirement-savings vehicle funded by your wages. Your employer may match part of your contributions, but even this match is considered additional wages.

Because you are not taxed on wages that go in the 401(k) plan, you are taxed when you withdraw money from your 401(k) plan. The way the IRS views it, wages go in and wages come out. So you may not be paying income taxes on the wages you contribute to a 401(k) plan, but you do pay income taxes on wages you withdraw.

And you pay them on both the federal and state level, most likely (unless you're lucky enough to live in a state with no income taxes).

And therein lies the problem. No matter how you invest, all the money in your 401(k) plan will eventually be taxed as income—and other than the federal estate tax, the income tax is the highest you can pay.

401(k) Lies Exposed

Lie #1: A 401(k) will keep your income taxes low.
Truth: A 401(k) doesn't lower income taxes—it simply defers them.

Lie #2: Your beneficiary can inherit your 401(k) tax efficiently.
Truth: Your beneficiary will pay every penny in taxes that you would have paid.

Lie #3: A 401(k) will keep your income taxes low.
Truth: A 401(k) converts a low-or no-tax event to a high tax event.

Capital Gains (and Losses)

Capital gains are profits realized from the sale of a capital asset. Common capital assets are businesses, real estate, works of art, and investments. But, according to the IRS, "almost everything you own and use for personal or investment purposes is a capital asset," including "personal-use items like household furnishings."

Sometimes when you sell an asset, you receive more for it than you originally paid for it. In this case, you have a capital gain. So if you buy a used car today for $10,000 and sell it tomorrow for $15,000, you have a $5,000 capital gain. Similarly, if you buy a stock today for $50 per share and sell it next week for $100 per share, you have a $50-per-share capital gain.

Of course, we always don't make such wise decisions. If you are unfortunate enough to receive less for a capital asset than you paid for it, you experience a capital loss. Consider the car example above.

If you buy a used car today for $10,000, but realize it is a lemon and dispose of it for $9,000, you have a $1,000 capital loss.

Taxation of Capital Gains: The Basics

What you paid for an asset is often, in accounting lingo, referred to as its basis. That may sound complicated, but we can simplify it. Basis is simply what you paid for an asset, plus any other costs you incurred to acquire it, including sales taxes, commissions, shipping and handling costs, and installation charges. It also includes the cost of improvements. So if you buy a house for $100,000 and spend $50,000 improving it, your basis is $150,000. (Depreciation of an asset, on the other hand, can reduce your basis. But we do not need to go into detail about that here.)

So how are capital gains taxed? First, you have to decide if the capital gain is long term or short term. If you hold the asset for more than one year before you dispose of it, your capital gain or loss is long term. If you hold the asset one year or less, your capital gain or loss is short term. To determine how long you held the asset, simply begin counting from the day after you acquired the asset, up to and including the day you disposed of the asset.

The reason the length of time you held an asset is important is because long-term and short-term capital gains are taxed at different rates. Short-term capital gains are taxed at the same rate as ordinary income. Long-term capital gains are taxed at a much lower rate. The table below illustrates.

Taxation of Long-Term Capital Gains

Income Tax Rate	Capital Gains Tax Rate
10%, 12%	0%
22%, 24%, 32%	15%
35%, 37%	20%

Why are capital gains taxed lower than ordinary income taxes, you might ask? It is because the government wants citizens to be long-term investors. Investment helps drive the economy forward, and benefits everyone, the theory goes.

Finally, note that while there is a difference between dividends and capital gains, the tax treatment is currently similar. In the past, common stock dividends were taxed at ordinary income tax rates. When the Jobs and Growth Tax Relief Reconciliation Act of 2003 was passed, however, dividends began receiving the same tax treatment as long-term capital gains. That led many companies to implement or raise dividends to make their stocks more appealing.

Why Do I Pay Capital Gains Tax When I Didn't Sell My Fund?

It is a common question from mutual fund investors. You held your mutual fund throughout the year, but your fund company still sends you a capital gains tax report come January. Why? Mutual funds consist of many different stocks or bonds. During the year, the fund manager buys and sells securities. Some of these transactions result in gains and others in losses. At the end of the year, if there is a net capital gain on what the portfolio manager sold, that gain is passed on to shareholders.

Offsetting Capital Gains with Losses

Any investment professional can (and should) tell you that investments do not always rise in value. Sometimes they fall. As noted earlier, in this case you have a capital loss. And capital losses can be deducted from capital gains in the case of investments.

As an example, if you have $10,000 in long-term gains from the sale of one investment, but $3,000 in long-term losses from the sale of another, you only have to pay taxes only on $7,000 worth of long-term capital gains.

You can offset up to $3,000 of capital gains per year with capital losses. If you have more than $3,000 in capital losses in any given year, you can carry them forward indefinitely, until you have used them all.

Now, there are some nuances to capital gains taxes, as is usually the case with investments. For example, capital gains on artwork and collectibles are taxed as ordinary income, up to a maximum rate of 28%. You may also exclude up to 50% of capital gains on stock held for more than five years in a domestic C corporation with gross assets under $50 million on the date of the stock's issuance. But let's not get into the nitty-gritty; that is an accountant's forte.

401(k) Plans and Capital Gains

One caveat regarding capital gains and losses pertains to 401(k) plans. If you realize a capital gain inside a 401(k), it is not taxed as a capital gain. It is taxed at the usually higher ordinary income tax rate when you withdraw it. Additionally, if you realize a capital loss in a 401(k), you cannot offset it against a capital loss as you would be able to outside a 401(k).

Let's make that simple with an example. Say Jane invests $10,000 into a growth fund outside a 401(k) plan, and Bob invests $10,000 into the same growth fund inside his 401(k) plan.

What happens if the value of the fund rises to $13,000, and Jane and Bob sell at the exact same time? Jane pays a capital gains tax of 0% to 20% on the $3,000 profit, depending on her income-tax bracket. Bob doesn't pay *any* capital gains now, but pays income tax on the earnings (10% to 37%) later, when he withdraws the money from his 401(k) plan.

Now, what happens if the value of the fund falls to $7,000, and Jane and Bob sell at the exact same time? Jane gets a tax deduction she can use against her income. Bob gets nothing but less money in retirement, when he starts to make withdrawals from his 401(k) plan.

Who got the better deal? I say Jane—because in essence, by investing via a 401(k) plan, you are eliminating the lower capital gains tax and replacing it with the much higher income tax.

Why You Have Been Swindled

Let's say you make an investment in your 401(k) plan, and believe—because you have been told so—that any gain you realize will not be exposed to capital-gains tax because it occurred inside your 401(k) plan. You have been misled. It is true that you will not have to pay capital-gains taxes on profitable investments made inside a 401(k) plan. But material information has been omitted. What would have been a capital gain had the investment occurred outside a 401(k) plan is now earned income, and taxable at the much higher federal tax rate (and state tax rate)! Capital gains, meanwhile, are not taxed at the state level in any single state.

Your Home: Exempt from Capital Gains?

Most Americans' largest single asset is their home. Depending on how long you own a home and how the real-estate market performed during that time, you might realize a significant capital gain on its sale. The good news: you can exclude up to $250,000 of the capital gain on your home sale if you are single, $500,000 if you are married filing jointly—provided certain conditions are met. First, you must have owned the home for at least two years in the five-year period before the sale. Second, the home must have been your primary residence for at least two years in that same five-year period. Finally, you cannot have excluded the capital gain from another home sale in the two-year period before the sale.

Business Income versus Capital Gains

If you operate a business, you may be tempted to report your business income as a capital gain. But it is not. Say you buy old furniture, spiff it up, and sell it on Etsy. While the money you pay for the old furniture is a business expense, the money you receive in sales in revenue, and the difference between the two is considered income. Your profit is therefore subject to income tax, not capital gains tax.

Managing Taxes with Tax-Managed Funds

Everyone wants to get ahead of Uncle Sam, and if you're an investor, one way to do so (legally) is to invest in tax-managed mutual funds.

Taxation Basics

The reason pertains to how mutual funds are taxed.

When you think of paying taxes in your mutual fund investments, you're probably thinking of capital gains taxes levied on your own sale of shares of the fund.

When you sell your mutual fund shares for more than you paid for them, you realize either a short-term or a long-term capital gain.

But there's another kind of tax when it comes to mutual funds: embedded gains that are distributed to shareholders each year. Inside of the mutual fund, the portfolio manager is constantly buying and selling securities. When a portfolio manager buys and sells securities at a gain, the mutual fund incurs a tax bill, and those taxes are passed on the shareholders (you) at the end of the year.

That's true even if you have all of your capital gains and dividends reinvested.

That's true even if you've only owned the fund for a short period of time.

Say it isn't so!

It's so. Let's say you invested last week and have all gains and dividends reinvested. Well, the mutual fund may have purchased a stock a long time ago, and now it sells that stock. You participate in your proportional share of the capital gain, so you also owe taxes on that gain.

That's right—even if you didn't sell and fund shares, you will still receive a 1099 form which shows the amount of your gain, and you will have to report the gain on your tax return and pay the applicable taxes.

Sometimes, your mutual fund can be down for the year, and you'll still owe taxes because of the trading activity in the portfolio—a bit of a double punch in the gut.

Enter Tax-Managed Funds

At some point in history, someone figured out that investors don't like that, and invested the tax-managed or tax-efficient mutual fund. These funds are designed to minimize the tax liability that shareholders face.

With a tax-managed mutual fund, the portfolio manager seeks to minimize capital gains distributions in a number of ways. He or she may minimizing the fund's turnover, especially if the fund invests in stocks. Stocks held for more than one year are taxed at a lower long-term capital gains rate. Typically, when the fund manager sells an investment at a profit (gain) they try to match it up with a corresponding loss. This technique will neutralize the gain thus eliminating the taxes due.

If you compare tax-managed mutual funds to the typical actively managed mutual fund, they are, indeed, dramatically more tax-efficient.

Where to Find Tax-Managed Funds

Many mutual funds companies offer funds that are designated as tax-managed.

Vanguard Tax-Managed Capital Appreciation Fund has $10.2 billion in assets under management as of 3/31/19. The portfolio's benchmark is the domestic Russell 1000 Index, though portfolio managers can make adjustments for dividend levels and other tax factors, such as taking advantage of losses. The turnover is 6.1%, and the expense ratio is 0.09%. And since the fund was launched in 2001, there has never been a capital gains distribution. (Other tax-managed Vanguard options include **Vanguard Tax-Managed Small Cap Fund** and **Vanguard Tax-Managed Balanced Fund.**)

Vanguard Tax-Managed Balanced Fund is another Vanguard option if you're looking for a mix of stocks and bonds. lt provides exposure to the mid- and large-cap segments of the U.S. stock market with about 50% of its assets, investing the balance in federally tax-exempt municipal bonds. The fund has $4.9 billion in assets under management as of 3/31/19, and its expense ratio is just 0.09%.

T. Rowe Price Tax-Efficient Equity Fund has $434 million in assets under management as of 3/31/19. More growth-oriented than the Vanguard fund, the portfolio's benchmark is the Russell 3000 Growth Index, and the fund expects to have significant investments in technology companies. The turnover is 0.2%, and the expense ratio is 0.8%.

Fidelity Tax-Free Bond is a good option if you're in the market for a bond fund. It holds municipal bonds, which are exempt from federal income tax. While municipal bonds generally have lower yields than corporate bonds, the tax-free status can produce a tax-effective yield that can beat other bonds. Generally, investors who are in higher tax brackets benefit the most from holding municipal bond funds. The fund has $3.8 billion in assets under management as of 3/31/19, and its expense ratio is 0.25%.

Russell Tax-Managed U.S. Large Cap Fund is another big one, with $3.2 billion in assets under management as of 3/31/19. A core fund (a blend of growth and value), it invests in other funds whose managers have inherently tax-sensitive investment approaches. If you like that idea, Russell has several other offerings that use the same multi-manager approach, including **Russell Tax-Managed U.S. Mid & Small Cap Fund** and **Russell Tax-Managed International Equity Fund.**

Blackrock iShares ETFs are an option if you prefer to go the route of index funds or ETFs, discusses in "Cons" above. Blackrock has more than 800 ETFs globally (more than 300 in the United States) and more than $1.5 trillion in ETF assets under management as of 3/31/19, so there's sure to be an iShares ETF for you. And over a five-year period ending 12/31/17, 58% of mutual funds paid out a capital gain distibution, versus 97% of non- ETFs and just 7% of iShares ETFs, according to Blackrock.

To determine how much you will save in a tax-managed fund versus other funds, you can review the mutual fund's statistics regarding a fund's historic tax costs.

Stepping Up in Basis

One more thing worth exploring when discussing the capital gains tax is gifts. The basis for an asset you received as a gift is equivalent to the donor's basis. So if your parents buy a cottage for $80,000, then give it to you ten years later when it is valued at $120,000, the basis is still $80,000.

But what about inheritances? Aha! That is different. The basis of an inherited asset is "stepped up" to the value of the asset on the date of the donor's death. So if your parents buy a cottage for $80,000, then die when it is valued at $120,000, at which point you inherit it, your basis is $120,000.

Why is there a discrepancy between gifts and inheritances? Uncle Sam is being nice. The provision of the tax code that allows inheritances to be treated differently essentially exempts from taxes any gains on assets held until someone's death.

The step-up in basis is a commonly overlooked tax benefit that can help minimize taxes. While gifting is often the preferred means of transferring wealth, you may want to be wary of gifting significantly appreciated assets during your lifetime, as it could result in capital gains taxes. These taxes could be avoided by allowing the assets to be transferred as an inheritance.

Consider how the step-up in basis might apply to investments. Say you purchase a share of stock for $1, and the value grows to $100, at which time you sell it. You would be responsible for paying capital gains tax on the $99 gain you received from this sale. Now, let's say instead of selling the stock, you die and leave it to your child when it is worth $100. Your child gets a new cost basis of $100. If he or she then sells the stock for $100, there is no capital gain. Your child has received the stock tax free. The step-up in basis erased the capital gains and the tax liability that would have accompanied it.

In summary, the step-up in basis is a simple concept. If you received a capital asset from another person because of his or her death, the cost basis (in essence, what the deceased paid for it) is the value of the asset at the time of the death. I believe it is the single biggest tax break in the entire tax code.

But it is never simple when it comes to taxes, is it? In some cases, a half step-up can apply. Let's say two spouses purchased stock for $50,000 and held it as joint tenants with rights of survivorship. One spouse passes away, at which time the stock is worth $100,000. In this case, a partial increase in basis may apply. The new basis for the surviving spouse would be equal to the fair market value on the date of death ($100,000) plus the original basis ($50,000) divided by two—so $75,000. In other words, half of the assets receive a stepped-up basis. But it may be best to leave that one to an accountant.

No Step-Up for 401(k)s

I believe the step-up in basis is the single biggest tax break in the entire tax code—but it doesn't apply to 401(k) plans, which is another reason to avoid them. If you are like most Americans, most of your retirement assets are held in 401(k) plans or Individual Retirement Account (IRAs). The assets held in a tax-deferred retirement plan such as these do not receive a step-up in cost basis. That is because all distributions from tax-deferred retirement plans—to you or to a beneficiary—are taxed as ordinary income.

Strategies for Gifting Qualified Retirement Assets

If you are charitably inclined, you may want to consider leaving gifts with income-tax liabilities (such as 401(k) or IRA assets) to a qualified charity. That is because such charities do not pay any taxes on gifts they receive, so your gift will go further than it would if it were left to someone who would have to pay taxes on it.

Another option for minimizing taxes on gifts with income-tax liabilities is leaving them to your spouse. Your surviving spouse can treat qualified retirement asset as if it is part of his or her own retirement account, deferring distributions (and income taxes) until he or she is seventy and a half years old (when individuals are required to begin taking their required minimum distributions from qualified retirement plans).

If you leave your qualified retirement plan to another individual, such as an adult child, he or she will be required to begin taking required minimum distributions from the plan *immediately*. If your child is in a high income-tax bracket, your gift will be diminished substantially by income taxes.

Taxes, Taxes, Everywhere

During its first 26 years of existence, the federal tax code only grew from 400 to 504 pages, according to Wolters Kluwer, CCH. It ballooned to 8,200 pages during World War II, and 26,300 pages in 1984. Now, as noted earlier, it is 74,608 pages long.

No wonder taxes are so complicated. But it helps to think of them in basics: income taxes or capital gains taxes. Hopefully we have provided a simple outline.

But don't you wish you could find a way to structure your retirement so at your death your loved ones will not be hit with a huge income-tax bill? There is, and I will talk about that later in this book.

Chapter XII

Tax Cuts and Jobs Act of 2017

One important feature of the new tax law is that it doubles the standard tax deduction to $12,000 per filer ($24,000 per couple). This means that the first $12,000 of income-any income-is federally tax free. If your total annual income is $12,000, you pay zero in federal taxes. This deduction is available to ALL tax filers. Warren Buffet doesn't pay one penny in taxes on the first $12,000 he earns each year. Yes, I realize he hits that cap within hours of the new year, but understanding how to use this deduction is one of the points of this book. I will talk about it more later.

To K-1 or Not to K-1, That Is the Question

While the main theme of this book is to expose the lies you've been told about 401(k) plans, my work would be incomplete if I didn't address the lies you've been told about retirement plans for small businesses. In this chapter, I'll show you a better way to save money for retirement while using the tax code to its full benefit.

Retirement Plan Basics

Let's start at the beginning. As a small business owner, you don't have the luxury of an employer-sponsored retirement plan to help ensure your financial future, and a traditional 401(k) plan is likely out of your reach given the administrative hassles associated with creating and maintaining one. But you do have some options. Let's review the most popular retirement plans for small businesses: the SIMPLE 401(k), the Self-Employed 401(k), the SIMPLE IRA, and the SEP IRA.

Savings Incentive Match Plan (SIMPLE) 401(k)

The SIMPLE 401(k) is an alternative to the traditional 401(k) for companies that have fewer than one hundred employees. Employees can elect to contribute up to $18,500 in 2018. As an employer, you must either (a) match each employee's contribution on a dollar-for-dollar basis up to 3% of the employee's compensation, or (b) make nonelective contributions of 2% of the employee's compensation up to an annual limit of $275,000 in 2018. If you choose to make nonelective contributions, you must make them for all eligible employees, whether or not they make contributions themselves.

Pros: The administrative burden of operating a SIMPLE 401(k) is significantly lower than that of a traditional 401(k) plan. Although you must file Form 5500 with the IRS each year, you aren't obligated to conduct costly nondiscrimination testing, which you would if you operated a traditional 401(k) plan.

Cons: Contributions vest immediately, negating the employee-retention benefit of a staged vesting plan.

Best for: Businesses that want 401(k) features with less hassle, and are willing to make contributions on behalf of employees.

Self-Employed 401(k)

If you're self-employed (or your only employee is your spouse), you can establish a self-employed 401(k), which is sometimes called a solo 401(k). A self-employed 401(k) allows you to maximize contributions because it considers you both employer and employee. As an employee, you can contribute up to 100% of your compensation up to an annual maximum $18,500 in 2018 ($24,500 if you're fifty or older). As an employer, you can contribute as much as 25% of your compensation up to an annual maximum of $55,000. Total contributions from both the employer and employee cannot be more than $55,000 in 2018.

Pros: For incorporated businesses, contributions are considered business expenses; for unincorporated business, contributions are deducted from personal income.

Cons: It doesn't cover employees. A plan administrator is required, and once plan assets reach $250,000, you'll have to file Form 5500 with the IRS.

Best for: Businesses without employees who want to maximize contributions.

Simplified Employee Pension (SEP) IRA

SEP IRAs are employer-funded retirement plans; employees make no contributions. In 2018, the contributions you make to each employee's SEP IRA (including your own) cannot exceed the lesser of 25% of compensation or $55,000. If you're self-employed, there's a special calculation to determine contributions for yourself. It's tricky, as the salary of the account holder is calculated after the contribution is made.

Pros: The plan is easy to set up and maintain, and there are no setup fees or annual charges. It also covers employees.

Cons: While you as an employer are not required to make a contribution every year, you must contribute the same percentage for employees that you contribute for yourself.

Best for: Businesses with employees who don't want employee participation.

SIMPLE IRA

With the SIMPLE IRA, businesses with fewer than one hundred employees can establish an IRA for each employee. Employees can make pretax contributions as high as 100% of their compensation, up to $12,500 in 2018 ($15,000 if you're fifty or older). As an employer, you must also contribute. You can either (a) match each employee's contribution on a dollar-for-dollar basis up to 3% of the employee's compensation, or (b) make nonelective contributions of 2% of the employee's compensation up to an annual limit of $275,000 in 2018.

Pros: The plan is easy to create and administer, and has more generous contribution limits than traditional and Roth IRAs.

Cons: Employee contributions are lower than that of the SIMPLE 401(k), and contributions are counted for the purposes of individual's overall annual limit on so-called elective deferrals (see sidebar).

Best for: Business with employees who want employee participation.

Why Use a Small Business Retirement Plan?

Qualified retirement plans such as these benefit employees and employers alike. As an employee, any contributions you make are excluded from your taxable income. The money you put into a plan grows tax deferred until you retire. Then, distributions, including earnings, are includible in your taxable income. As an employer, your contributions to qualified retirement plans are generally deducted against your business's income. It can get complicated, as anything having to do with taxes can, but that's all we need to know before we move on.

Pass-Through Income Explained

Now, thanks to the Tax Cuts and Jobs Act, there's another way to reduce your business's taxable income. But before we explain how, we need to ensure you understand the basics of pass-through income.

That's a term you may never have heard of before. It's used by the Internal Revenue Service (IRS) to explain how taxes are calculated for certain entities.

The official definition of a pass-through entity is a business entity that is not taxed at the entity level. In other words, it passes its income, losses, deductions, and credits on to its owners. The owners may be partners, shareholders, beneficiaries, or investors.

But we can simplify that. Think about it this way.

C corporations—which are most large US corporations—are subject to double taxation. Money that flows into a C corporation is first taxed at the business level. When the C corporation distributes leftover income to the shareholder, the shareholder pays taxes on it too.

Smaller businesses are taxed differently. You probably know that all small businesses have owners; most have several owners. When the business earns a profit, *the business* doesn't pay taxes on that profit. Instead, the profit is *passed through* to the business owners, who include it on their personal tax returns as ordinary income. So if my business has a $25,000 profit, it will send the IRS and me a Schedule K-1 showing the $25,000 profit. I will add that $25,000 to my income in that tax year and pay income taxes at my individual tax rate.

The IRS defines a pass-through entity as follows: a partnership that has not elected to be classified as a C corporation; an S corporation; a joint venture; a real estate mortgage investment conduit (REMIC); a limited liability company (LLC) that has more than one member and has not elected to be classified as a corporation; or any other business entity that is not a trust or corporation and has not elected to be classified as a C corporation.

What the IRS Giveth, It Taketh Away

Let's look at an example. Say you sit down with your certified public accountant (CPA) to do your taxes. She tells you your small business earned a $10,000 profit for the year. Although you're excited, you may be concerned about the taxes that will be due on this windfall.

According to the IRS, your business is required to send you, as the business owner, a Schedule K-1. This form is distributed by small businesses to its owners as a means of reporting the business's profits or losses for the prior tax year.

In this case, as the sole owner of your business, you will receive a Schedule K-1 in the amount of $10,000. Your CPA will add this $10,000 to your other income, and you will pay taxes on it as ordinary income tax rates—as high as 37% starting in 2018.

As any good CPA would do, yours explains that there is a way to defer paying taxes on the $10,000—by opening a small business retirement plan such as those I've described previously and contributing your $10,000 profit to the plan. Poof! Your income will be offset by the contribution. You decide to take your CPA's advice.

How good was this simple tax maneuver? If you're in the 22% federal income-tax bracket, you saved $2,200. So you're happy, and your CPA is happy. You shake her hand and leave, and go about your business as usual.

This scenario occurs millions of times per year in this country, and every time it occurs it's a mistake. Why? Because the conversation wasn't finished. You and your CPA didn't discuss what happens when you retire and start to withdraw the money you put into your small business retirement plan.

As I've said time and time again, every time the IRS gives you something, it takes something away. In this example, the IRS gave you a $2,200 tax deduction—$2,200 of real money that is in your pocket today. I'm now going to explain what you gave up for that $2,200.

Tax Cuts and Jobs Act of 2017

Now, thanks to the Tax Cuts and Jobs Act of 2017, which went into effect in January 2018, there's another way to reduce your business's taxable income.

The new law allows pass-through entities to take a deduction of 20% against their business income. This essentially reduces the effective top rate on pass-through entities' income by roughly 10 percentage points over pre-2018 tax law.

Of course, nothing that involves taxes is ever easy. Claiming the new 20% deduction requires navigating a tangle of barely comprehensible requirements and limitations that make it far from guaranteed accessible to small business owners.

Basically, anyone who generates "qualified business income" will be entitled to take a deduction of 20% of that qualified business income on their tax return, which sounds simple. But, the deduction is equal to the sum of (1) the lesser of (a) the "combined qualified business income" of the taxpayer *or* (b) 20% of the excess of taxable income over the sum of any net capital gain, *plus* (2) the lesser of 20% of qualified cooperative dividends *or* taxable income less net capital gain.

Is your head spinning yet? That's tax law for you.

There are also income thresholds: single filers who earn less than $157,500 and married filers who earn less than $315,000 may take the deduction no matter what business they're in. After taxable income passes those thresholds, however, the law limits who can take the deduction. Specifically, individuals operating service businesses—such as doctors, lawyers, and financial advisors—may not be able to take the deduction if their income is greater than the threshold.

A (Hopefully) Simple Example

Let's provide a simple example. Imagine that you're a sole proprietor, so you're a pass-through entity. Your business income and expenses are reported on your individual federal form 1040, Schedule C.

Your business has a gross income of $130,000 and expenses of $30,000, so you have a net profit of $100,000. This is your qualified business income.

Your spouse, meanwhile, also works, earning $70,000 per year.

So your joint income is $170,000 (below the threshold for joint filers, I'll add). Your standard deduction is $24,000, you have above-the-line deductions of $7,500 for the deductible portion of your self-employment tax, and you made $20,000 for SEP IRA contributions. That means your taxable income is $118,500.

Your taxable income of $118,500 is greater than your qualified business income of $100,000, so the 20% pass-through deduction would apply to your qualified business income, resulting in a $20,000 deduction.

You would save about $4,400 in federal taxes. How did I calculate that?

As a couple, you are in the 22% tax bracket.

Without the 20% deduction, you would pay 22% taxes on $118,500, or $26,070.

With the tax deduction, you would pay 22% taxes on $98,500 ($118,500 minus your $20,000 deduction), or $21,670.

$26,070 minus $21,670 is $4,400.

Let's not go into much more detail about the requirements and limitations, that being the province of accountants. Here, I'd simply like to follow the money.

A Better Option? Let's Follow the Money

Here's the $100,000 question then: Instead of putting money in a retirement plan, are you better off keeping it and using the new 20% deduction? Let's look at this option in more detail, so put on your small-business hat.

Let's take two small business owners who each have a $10,000 profit at the end of the year. We'll call them Mr. SEP IRA (SEP) and Mrs. Schedule K-1 (K-1).

Mr. SEP decides to contribute his $10,000 business profit to a SEP IRA, while Mrs. K-1 decides to take the money as income, thereby ensuring she will receive a Schedule K-1 from the IRS. And, they both put the money in exactly the same investment on exactly the same day.

As a sidenote, it may seem strange to you that you can invest in exactly the same investment both inside and outside of a retirement plan, but it's true. Investments—stocks, bonds, mutual funds, and such—are not designated as retirement or non-retirement investments. The only difference is the type of account: taxable (non-retirement account) or tax-deferred (retirement account). This means you can invest the money in your retirement account in virtually anything under the sun—real estate, gold, art, jewelry, even classic cars. So when I say Mr. SEP and Mrs. K-1 put their $10,000 in exactly the same investment, not only is it true—but also it's something the wealthy people in this country do every day.

Let's assume, however, that Mr. SEP and Mrs. K-1 invested their $10,000 in the Vanguard S&P 500 Index Fund (VFINX). I'm not advocating for index funds; this is simply a choice that will prevent the outcome from being swayed by investment performance, which is important because this entire exercise is intended to show how taxes impact your retirement.

How does Mr. SEP IRA fare?

He deposits $10,000 into a SEP IRA and invests it in VFINX.

His assumed tax bracket is 22%, so he pays $2,200 in taxes today.

After ten years the SEP IRA has grown to $22,189.

Mr. SEP retires, and all distributions from his SEP IRA are taxed as ordinary income at a rate between 10% and 37% (under current tax law, anyway).

Let's assume in retirement, Mr. SEP is in the 10% income-tax bracket, so he pays 10% tax on that $22,189, or $2,218.90. His net: $19,970.10.

There is no way around this. Even if Mr. SEP dies before or during his retirement, his beneficiary will be obligated to pay income taxes on his or her inheritance.

How does Mrs. K-1 fare?

Since her $10,000 is considered business income, Mrs. K-1 gets a 20% tax deduction on it, meaning she only pays taxes on $8,000. Because her assumed tax bracket is also 22%, she pays $1,760 in taxes today.

Mrs. K-1 deposits the balance—$8,240—in a taxable brokerage account and invests it in VFINX.

After ten years the brokerage account has grown to $18,283.

Mrs. K-1 retires. How are distributions from her brokerage account taxed?

First, she can withdraw the money she already paid taxes on—$8,000—tax free. The remaining balance of $10,283 is taxed as long-term capital gain at a rate of 0% because, like Mr. SEP, Mrs. K-1 is in the 10% income-tax bracket in retirement.

Yes, you read that right: Mrs. K-1 pays no capital-gains tax. The capital-gains tax ranges from 10% to 20%, and taxpayers in the 10% and 15% income-tax brackets pay no tax on long-term gains on most assets.

So Mrs. K-1 nets $18,283. That's still less than Mr. SEP, you might say, but Mrs. K-1 has some other advantages over Mr. SEP. She doesn't need to take required minimum distributions (RMDs) from her brokerage account, as Mr. SEP does from his SEP IRA. She can also offset her capital gain with capital losses without limit (versus income taxes, which can only be offset with $3,000 of capital losses per year). Finally—and perhaps most importantly—if Mrs. K-1 dies, the balance of her account goes to her heirs free of any income or capital gains taxes.

The Moral of the Story

As promised, I've showed you a better way to invest small business profits that would ordinarily be earmarked for a retirement plan.

The moral of the story? Don't be seduced by short-term benefits. That's what Uncle Sam is banking on.

Instead, I challenge you to look at the big picture—past the pennies you can save today and instead at the dollars you could save in the future. Don't you want to retire as tax free as possible?

I'm always preaching to my clients that the difference between the rich and the rest of us is that the rich know how to work the tax code in their favor. After all, it's the rich who send our lawmakers to Washington, DC, with one main objective: keep the tax code complex so the middle class keeps paying for the poor.

Now you know one of their secrets. Let's keep it between us.

Chapter XIII

The Smart 401(k)

> Why aren't you signed up for the 401K? I'd never be able to run that far.
>
> —Scott Adams, Dilbert, May 2, 2001

> A lot of people become pessimists from financing optimists.
>
> —C. T. Jones

In my first book, *The Money Compass*, the chapter that got the most attention was the one on 401(k) plans. My readers couldn't believe their 401(k) plans were their biggest tax generators for Uncle Sam. But it's true. The system is designed, or rigged if you want to call it that, to trap you into a loop of never-ending taxes. As I've said during my TV interviews, "The rich pass laws to make the middle class subsidize the poor." This is just one the reason we are witnessing the destruction of the middle class. But I digress. Let's talk about 401(k) plans.

The Ins and Outs of 401(k) Plans

In this chapter I will show you how to use the 3 important tax laws to create a TAX-FREE retirement and estate. Keep in mind, I am writing this for the 99% of us not in the top 1%. They "earned" out of this option many billions of dollars ago. That's why they have a team of lawyers/CPA's. You and I don't have that "problem." My techniques are designed for the rest of us who just want to improve their financial lives and make sure we are applying all the current tax code properly.

The Smart 401(k) comes down to following 3 simple IRS rules:

Rule #1: Standard Deduction ($12,000 Annual Tax Free Max)

We all get $12,000 of tax-free income a year. The problem is we all use it to reduce our taxes today by a small amount. How much? For most of us, it's approximately $100 per month. I say, go out to dinner once less a month and apply that deduction to your retirement years. In fact, the proof that my logic is sound is the rise of Roth 401(k)'s. A Roth 401(k) is funded by after-tax dollars. The Smart 401 (k) is like a Roth 401 (k) on steroids.

Rule #2: Distribution, Capital Gains ($38,600 Annual Tax Free Max)

By applying your standard deduction each year to your retirement savings and investing it in a tax-managed account, you will now be able to withdraw money using the capital gain tax rates. This mean, you can withdraw (in this example) $36,000 from your account. For the first $12,000 you can apply your standard deduction, and the remaining $24,000 is taxed at the capital gain rate. Your total federal taxes due: $0 (zero).

Rule #3: At Death, Step-up in Basis ($11.4 Million Life Tax Free Max)

The step-up rule is the golden goose for the rich. It simply means that you can pass aftertax appreciated assets to your heirs tax free. The 2019 limit on this exemption is $11.4 million per person. No problem!!!

So, to review:

1. Use your standard deduction to "fund" your after-tax retirement account.

2. Invest it in special tax-managed mutual funds. Pull money out tax free (limit applies) as needed.
3. Pass on to heirs, using the step-up in basis.

For 99% of us, I just showed you how to save TAX FREE, withdraw TAX FREE, and pass it on TAX FREE.

Today, the old-school retirement plans known as defined-benefit plans or pensions are rare.

401(k) plans—which allow employees to contribute funds to a qualified retirement plan via a pretax reduction in salary—have been a staple of retirement saving since they were created by the Revenue Act of 1978 and went into effect on January 1, 1980. There are other similar tax-deductible plans for nonprofit organizations, but all are designed to create an incentive for retirement saving by deferring wage earners' income taxes until a future date.

It's easy to understand why 401(k) plans are so attractive. They allow employees to save up to $18,000 a year, pretax, and direct the manner in which it's invested (with an additional $6,000 catch-up contribution allowed for those age fifty and older). Earnings derived from the investments in the plan are not taxed; they're reinvested, and compound over time.

In 2006, a new type of 401(k) plan became available: the Roth. Roth 401(k) plans allow wage earners to contribute *after-tax* funds to a retirement plan. Contributions have already been taxed, so withdrawals of those contributions in retirement are tax free (and there's the possibility that investment earnings could qualify for a nontaxable distribution as well). That offers another level of flexibility for individuals who want more spendable income in retirement.

With both traditional and Roth 401(k) plans, employees can invest in stocks, bonds, or combination of stocks and bonds, depending on the level of risk the employee can tolerate.

Adding to the appeal of 401(k) plans, many employers match part of an employee's contribution. According to Aon's *2015 Trends & Experience in DC Plans Survey*, 42% of companies match employees' 401(k) contributions dollar-for-dollar, up from 31% in 2013.

Another benefit of 401(k) plans is that they offer some flexibility if you're in a financial pinch. You have two options.

First, you can take a loan from your 401(k) plan, if permitted by the plan (and 87% of 401(k) plans offer loan options, according to the Employee Benefit Research Institute, or EBRI). Such loans typically allow you to borrow up to 50% of your account balance up to a maximum of $50,000. You must repay the loan within five years unless you're using the money for a down payment on a home, in which case the repayment period is longer. And typically, you repay the loan through automatic deductions from your paycheck. It's a great option if you need a loan, because instead of paying interest to a bank, you're paying it to yourself.

Second, IRS rules allow you to take what's called a hardship withdrawal from your 401(k) plan (though your employer has to allow it as well). Acceptable reasons for a hardship withdrawal, according to the IRS, are (1) unreimbursed medical expenses for you, your spouse, or dependents; (2) purchase of your principal residence; (3) payment of college tuition and related educational costs for you, your spouse, dependents, or children who are no longer dependents; (4) payments necessary to prevent eviction of you from your home, or foreclosure on the mortgage of your principal residence; (5) funeral expenses; and (6) certain expenses for the repair of damage to your principal residence. Such hardship withdrawals are subject to income tax and, if you are not at least fifty-nine and a half years of age, a 10% withdrawal penalty.

Hardship withdrawals are penalty free if you meet any one of a number of specific requirements—for example, you become totally disabled; you're in debt for medical expenses that exceed 7.5% of your adjusted gross income; or you're required by court order to pay funds to a spouse, child, or dependent. Other acceptable reasons for a penalty-free hardship withdrawal include (a) permanent layoff, termination, quitting, or early retirement in the same year you turn fifty-five; or (b) permanent layoff, termination, quitting, or retirement accompanied by payments for the rest of your (or your designated beneficiaries') life or life expectancy that continues for at least five years or until you reach age fifty-nine and a half, whichever is longer.

With such features, 401(k) plans are extremely popular. Many financial pundits—financial advisors, corporate human resources managers, and financial institutions—tout their advantages as a great way to save for retirement.

And individual investors listen. According to the most recent statistics from the US Department of Labor (as of April 2014), there are 638,390 defined contribution retirement plans in the United States, 513,000 of which are 401(k) plans. Nearly 80% of full-time workers have access to employer-sponsored retirement plans, and more than 80% of these workers participate in a plan.

One survey from the Plan Sponsor Council of America found that the average percentage of eligible employees with a balance in a defined-contribution plan is 87.6%.

As of the first quarter of 2016, US retirement assets in defined contribution plans were $6.8 trillion, of which $4.8 trillion were held in 401(k) plans, according to the Investment Company Institute (out of $24.1 trillion in total retirement assets).

But then there are the management fees.

*****

Wish I Had Thought about That

> I thought I was smart until I got my Fidelity 401(k) materials in the mail. It turns out that Fidelity Cash Reserves, the $118 billion money market fund where my cash is held, charges annual expenses of 0.31%. That's more than three times the 0.10% expense ratio Fidelity charges for its S&P 500 Index fund, which also happens to have yielded 1.9% during the past year compared to a 0.01% yield for cash reserves. (Scott Cendrowski, "Your Cash Is Costing You," CNN Money, February 20, 2012)

*****

The Truth about Your 401(Dismay)!

Hey—brace yourself, because the advice I'm about to give you may seem like financial heresy: stop contributing to your 401(k) plan immediately!

You read that right—and the reason is that investing in your 401(k) plan is a mistake that could cost you and your loved ones *hundreds of thousands of dollars in taxes.*

I've studied this topic extensively. So far, however, my theory hasn't gained any traction. I've spoken to clients, certified public accountants (CPAs), and even an IRS agent about it. One CPA looked me square in the eye and said, "You're nuts!"

Am I nuts or just not brainwashed?

Throughout our working lives, we've all been taught to save money for retirement via a 401(k) plan. The pitch goes something like this: You get a tax deduction today, and the money grows tax deferred. Then, when you withdraw the money in retirement, you'll likely be in a lower tax bracket. In the end, then, you reduce how much you pay in taxes.

What do I think about that argument? It's wrong! The problem with the traditional logic is that it doesn't tell you how things will work out in the end. It's like Evel Knievel telling you how easy it is to jump a motorcycle over fifty buses. The jumping is easy; it's the landing that can be very painful.

Similarly, when it comes to 401(k) plans, people generally talk about only the accumulation phase (the jump); no one is willing to talk about the distribution phase (the landing). I, however, am going to present you with both the jump and the landing—proving in the process that a 401(k) plan will generate more tax revenue for the IRS than an investment in an after-tax account. Hold on tight, because you're in for quite a ride. But I promise we will stick the landing.

Brief disclosure: there are more than one hundred million tax filers in the United States. Even though we all use the same tax code, just like snowflakes, there are no two tax returns that are identical. I guarantee you that there are many folks whose individual situation would make my approach fruitless. However, the vast majority of Americans would, no doubt, benefit from what I am about to present to you. Also, the following does not include the impact a company match would have on the outcome. My reason for this will follow in a later chapter.

So sit back in your most comfortable chair with your favorite beverage and open your mind because you're about to see behind the curtain of how the wealthy get that way—and just as importantly, *stay* that way.

Meet Mr. Uninformed and Mrs. Smart

To make my point, I'll run two different scenarios, one for Mr. Uninformed and one for Mrs. Smart. Both invested $1,000 per month from August 1979 until August 2009. Both invested in Vanguard 500 Index Fund (VFINX), a mutual fund that tracks the S&P 500 Index, so investment performance was identical. Both ended up with $1,781,538 in their accounts.

It should be noted that the 401(k) contribution limit in 1979 was below $12,000 annually. I chose the 1979–2009 time period because most retirees savings are the result of thirty years of building their nest egg.

However, Mr. Uninformed invested his money in a traditional 401(k) plan, and Mrs. Smart invested her money in an after-tax account, which is an account funded with after-tax dollars.

Here's where the fun begins.

Phase 1: Accumulation (Standard Deduction)

Under new tax laws the IRS allows all individual filers to deduct the first $12,000 of their earned income each year. Joint filers can deduct $24,000. So that means when Mr. Uninformed contributed the $1,000 a month ($12,000 annually) to his 401(k), this was money that wasn't going to be taxed anyway. But now it is in a tax-deferred account.

Mrs. Smart also used her $12,000 standard deduction to fund her after-tax account.

Let's summarize:

Mr. Uniformed put $12,000 into his 401(k) and paid $0 in taxes on the money. Now the $12,000 is in a tax-deferred account, so all growth on the money will be taxed as *income* when he withdraws it.

Mrs. Smart put $12,000 into her after-tax account and paid no taxes on the money. Now the $12,000 is in an after-tax account, so all growth on the money will be taxed as *capital gains* when she withdraws it.

Since both invested their contributions in the exactly same investment on the same day they ended up with exactly the amount of money. See table 6.1.

Table 6.1: Mr. Uniformed Meets Mrs. Smart

	Mr. Uninformed	**Mrs. Smart**
401(k) plan	$1,781,538	$0
Tax-managed after-tax account	$0	$ 1,781,358
Net value at retirement	$1,781,538	$1,781,538

So there is no winner, right? So far, it certainly looks that way, because if, by the time you retire, you have accumulated the same amount of money in a 401(k) plan than you would in an after-tax account, the 401(k) plan must be the best option, most people would say.

Phase 2: Distribution (Capital Gain)

But wait a moment. Let's look what happens as Mr. Uninformed and Mrs. Smart progress into retirement. Both investors start a systematic withdrawal program, taking $36,000 a year from their nest eggs. And here's where we begin to see a difference.

Mr. Uninformed withdraws $36,000 and receives a 1099-R at the end of the year. A 1099-R is a tax form used to report distributions from annuities, profit-sharing plans, retirement plans, IRAs, insurance contracts, and pension plans. It is required by the IRS from any individual who has a distribution of more than $10.

The 1099-R cues the IRS that Mr. Uninformed withdrew $36,000 from his 401(k) and he needs to add that to his current tax return. As with his contribution, the first $12,000 is deductible, thus tax free. That leaves Mr. Uninformed to pay ordinary income tax on the remaining $24,000. Table 6.2 shows his taxes due. Please note that all the income above these thresholds will be subject to ordinary income tax. However, the first $12,000 withdrawn are income and capital gain free.

Table 6.2: Mr. Uninformed's Tax Bill

	401(k) Plan
Withdrawal	$36,000
Standard deduction	$12,000
Taxable income	$24,000
Tax bracket	12%
Federal income tax due	$2,689.50

Meanwhile, Mrs. Smart withdraws the same $36,000 from her after-tax account. The same $12,000 deduction applies. However, her balance of $24,000 is taxed as capital gains, not as ordinary income. Table 6.3 shows her taxes due.

Table 6.3: Mrs. Smart's Tax Bill

	Tax-Managed Account
Withdrawal	$36,000
Standard deduction	$12,000
Taxable capital gain (at 0%)	$24,000
Taxable income	$0
Capital gains tax due	$0

Yes, you read that correctly. Mrs. Smart owes $0 in income tax and $0 in capital gains tax.

I know, most of you are saying that can't be correct. There is no way this is possible.

Well, America, it is correct, and it is possible!

How?

Not all capital gains are treated equally. The tax rate can vary dramatically between short-term and long-term gains.

Short-term capital gains—those on assets you have held for one year or less—do not benefit from any special tax rate. They are taxed at the same rate as your ordinary income.

Long-term capital gains—those on assets you have held for longer than a year—are reduced. The taxes are 0%, 15%, or 20% for most taxpayers, depending on their tax bracket. Mrs. Smart's tax bracket was low enough that she had a 0% tax rate on capital gains.

Mr. Uninformed, on the other hand, didn't receive this benefit. Whether you generate a short-term or long-term gain in a tax-advantaged account, you don't have to pay any tax until you take the money out of the account—but everything you withdraw, even profits from long-term capital gains, are taxable as ordinary income. Essentially, you obtain the benefit of tax deferral but lose the benefit of the long-term capital gains tax rate.

Phase 3: Death (Step-up in Basis)

Now, let's say ten years go by, and Mr. Uninformed and Mrs. Smart see their money grow by the same amount. Both make annual withdrawals of $36,000, and Mr. Uninformed pays roughly $28,800 ($2,880 times 10) on those withdrawals, while Mrs. Smart pays $0.

Then tragedy strikes, and both Mr. Uninformed and Mrs. Smart pass away. Upon their death, each has $1,781,538 left, and those funds are distributed to their beneficiaries, who, we will assume, are their children, and pay no estate taxes.

The distribution from Mr. Uninformed's account is considered income to his children, and that distribution is a taxable event. As a result, Mr. Uninformed's children are hit with a tax bill of $427,569 (assuming a tax bracket of 24% at the federal level and 0% at the state level). In the end, Mr. Uninformed children's net inheritance is only $1,327,075.

Now, let's look at what happens to Mrs. Smart's beneficiary, who, we will assume, are her children. She did not receive a 1099-R and gets to keep all the $1,781,538 in her account. Why? Because upon Mrs. Smart's death, her children get what is called a step-up in cost basis to the value of the account at the date of death—a provision that does not apply to retirement accounts such as Mr. Uninformed. That may sound complicated, but it simply refers to the adjustment of the cost of an appreciated asset, upon inheritance, for tax purposes. With a step-up in cost basis, the value of the asset is the market value of the asset at the time of inheritance, not the market value at which the asset was purchased—and the former is usually higher. As a result, Mrs. Smart's tax bill at death is $0, and her children nets $1,781,538.

Table 6.4: The Big Picture

	Mr. Uninformed	**Mrs. Smart**
Accumulation at death	$1,781,538	$1,781,538
Taxes paid at death	$427,569	$0
Net value at death	$1,327,075	$1,781,538
Difference		$454,463

So Mrs. Smart's beneficiary netted $454,463 more than Mr. Uninformed's beneficiary. Pretty good, right? Well, it gets even better for Mrs. Smart if you look at how much total she paid in taxes over the years relative to Mr. Uninformed.

Table 6.4: The Bigger Picture

	Mr. Uninformed	**Mrs. Smart**
Taxes paid during accumulation phase	$0	$0
Taxes paid during distribution phase	$28,800	$0
Taxes paid at death	$427,569	$0
Total taxes paid	**$456,449**	**$0**

You must be asking yourself, "How can this be? This isn't what I was told all these years." But there's a reason Mrs. Smart came out ahead. It's not because she possessed an incredible ability to manage the stock market. Remember, Mrs. Smart and Mr. Uninformed invested in *exactly* the same investments on *exactly* the same days. Mrs. Smart came out ahead because she understood the tax laws and how to use them to her advantage.

That reminds me of the time Warren Buffett, considered by most to be the greatest stock picker the world has ever known, said his secretary is in a higher tax bracket than he is. Now you know why he said that.

*****

Mrs. Smart's Capital Losses

Mrs. Smart has another advantage over Mr. Uninformed.

If your investments end up losing money rather than generating capital gains, you can use those losses to reduce your taxes.

You simply match up your gains and losses in any given year to determine your net capital gain or loss. If you end up with a net loss, you can use up to $3,000 per year to reduce your taxable income. If you have a net loss of more than $3,000, you can carry it forward to future tax years, to either offset capital gains or ordinary income.

But that's only possible in an after-tax account. Because you don't generate capital gains or losses in a retirement account, you can't use capital losses to offset capital gains or income.

*****

A Little More Sizzle

If that's not enough to convince you that investing in a 401(k) plan isn't a good idea, let's add some more sizzle to this steak. During both the accumulation and distribution phases—meaning before and after retirement—Mrs. Smart can withdraw money at any time from her account without paying a penny in income taxes, penalties, or excise taxes. So if Mrs. Smart needs to make a big purchase, or encounters some kind of financial hardship, such as significant medical bills, she can easily get to her money. Whether she needs $500 or $50,000, she can touch it at *any time* for *any reason.* Mr. Uninformed, however, has to jump through government-created hoops—which include claiming hardship, making in-service withdrawals, and taking loans—to touch the smallest amount of his money.

What About Loans?

But what about loans, you may ask. Mr. Uninformed could easily, if necessary, take a loan from his 401(k) plan to access his money.

Traditional wisdom holds that taking a loan from your own 401(k) plan is a good idea—because in doing so, you are actually paying yourself back with interest. And the interest rate is typically low, usually around the prime rate plus 1%.

But there are some difficulties with 401(k) plan loans. You typically have to borrow at least $1,000, and you usually can't borrow more than 50% of your account balance (to a maximum of $50,000). You can borrow only the vested amount, meaning your unvested company contributions are off-limits. The maximum loan term is five years. You generally cannot have more than one loan at a time, meaning you must borrow what you need the first time.

That's a lot of obstacles! And, even if you can overcome all of those obstacles, there will likely be a loan origination fee and annual administration fee. Then, if you are unable to pay back your loan, the IRS will view the unpaid balance as an early withdrawal and hit you with a 10% penalty.

What Catch-Up Contributions?

You may also wonder about catch-up contributions. Do they make investing in 401(k) plans more appealing?

Just to ensure we're on the same page, a 401(k) plan may permit participants who are age fifty or over at the end of a calendar year to make an elective contribution beyond the general limits that apply to 401(k) plans. These contributions are commonly referred to as catch-up contributions.

You may or may not be able to make a catch-up contribution because an employer is not required to provide for catch-up contributions in any of its plans.

However, if your plan does allow for catch-up contributions, here are the general rules: If you participate in a traditional or so-called safe harbor 401(k) plan, and you are age fifty or older, the catch-up contribution is $6,000 as of 2018. If you participate in a Savings Incentive Match Plan for Employees of Small Employers (SIMPLE) 401(k) plan, and you are age fifty or older, the catch-up contribution is $3,000 as of 2019.

Assuming you can make such contributions, is investing in a 401(k) plan still a bad idea? Yes, and for the same reasons I've already stated. Being able to contribute more money doesn't make a difference. A tax-managed account has no limits on contributions or on catch-up contributions. If you win the lottery, you can put as much as 100% of the windfall in a tax-managed account and multiply the benefits.

Another Reason to Watch Out: Automatic Enrollments

When left to their own devices, many employees don't contribute to their 401(k) plans, or they contribute just enough to qualify for matching funds their employers may offer, usually 6% or less.

That may not be enough to fund a solid retirement, since many financial planners say employees should aim to save at least 10% or more of their pretax earnings over their working lives to ensure an adequate retirement nest egg.

Indeed, a sizable percentage of US workers say they have virtually no money in retirement savings. According to the EBRI's 2016 *Retirement Confidence Survey*, 54% of US workers report that the total value of their household's savings and investments, excluding the value of their primary home and any defined-benefit plans, is less than $25,000. And about half of households age fifty-five and older have no retirement savings, according to a June 2015 report from the Government Accountability Office (GAO).

Why? People just aren't contributing to their 401(k) plans. While 53% of US workers are offered a plan by their current employer, just 45% say they contribute money, according to the EBRI's 2016 *Retirement Confidence Survey.* And according to the same EBRI survey, just 21% of US workers are "very confident" they'll have enough money saved for a comfortable retirement.

As a result, many employers automatically enroll employees in their 401(k) plans—i.e., they opt them in—thanks to the Pension Protection Act (PPA) of 2006, which removed many of the legal barriers to automatically enrolling eligible employees in such plans. According to Aon's *2015 Trends & Experience in DC Plans Survey*, 52% of employers automatically enroll workers at a savings rate of 4% or more, up from 39% of employers in 2013.

A similar feature is automatic escalation, in which a 401(k) plan, usually at the start of each year, automatically raises the percentage of pay that plan participants contribute by 1% or more, until they achieve a set deferral rate, such as 10%.

That doesn't mean employees give up their rights to enroll or not enroll, or how much to contribute; it just means that if they don't want to participate, or participate less, they have to opt out.

The data on opt-ins and opt-outs varies. According to a 2015 survey report by the Defined Contribution Institutional Investment Association (DCIIA), 62% of employers with large plans (more than $200 million in assets) automatically enroll new employees into their plan, while 48% of smaller employers do. But retirement services firm Ascensus says only 18% of the forty-thousand-plus retirement plans serviced by it automatically enroll their employees.

There's some evidence that automatic enrollment works. According to Ascensus, only around 1% of workers that are automatically enrolled into a retirement plan choose to opt out. That's one reason President Obama, when in office, proposed new rules around automatic enrollments. He wanted employers with more than ten workers to automatically enroll employees in an individual retirement account (IRA) if they didn't provide another type of retirement benefit. And he wanted to give companies with one hundred or fewer employees who did so a tax credit of up to $3,000. He didn't succeed. The legislative branch didn't take the bait.

But given the problems with 401(k) plans I've described above, do you really want to be enrolled without your consent?

One Exception

Now, you may have one more question. What if your company matches 401(k) plan contributions? Does that still mean investing in a 401(k) plan is a bad idea? First, fewer and fewer companies are matching 401(k) plan contributions these days. But if you're one of the lucky few employees who receives a match, the answer is that investing in a 401(k) plan isn't *quite* such a bad idea. But you should invest only up to the level of the company match. In other words, if your company matches up to 4%, contribute 4% and not a penny more.

Snapshot: Traditional 401(k) vs. Roth 401(k) vs. 1099(m) Plan

	Traditional 401(k)	**Roth 401(k)**	**1099(m)**
Eligibility Age	21	21	At birth
Contribution Limits	$19,000* *in 2019	$19,000* *in 2019	Unlimited
Catch-Up Contributions (Age 50-Plus)	$6,000* *in 2019	$6,000* *in 2019	Unlimited
Employer Match	Allowed, if offered by employer	Allowed, if offered by employer	Unavailable

Contribution Taxation Investment options Investment Advice	Pre-tax Limited to plan menu. Usually 10–20 Choices Limited	After-tax Limited to plan menu. Usually 10–20 Choices Limited	After-tax Unlimited Yes
Withdrawal Taxation	All with-drawals taxed as Income	Earnings taxed as Income before 5 years and under age 59 1/2	Taxed as Capital Gain Short term less than one year
Tax Rate Excise Tax	As Income Rates 12% to 32% 10% under age 59 1/2	As Income Rates 12% to 32% 10% under age 59 1/2 On growth	As Capital Gain Rates 0% to 20% Short Term Capital Gain rates same as Income 0%
Access	Not until age 59 1/2	Not until age 59 1/2 and have held account for more than five years	Anytime
Penalty-Free Distributions Before Age 59½	No	No	Yes

Required Minimum Distributions	Begin age 70 1/2 or when the account holder retires, whichever comes later	Begin age 70 1/2 or when the account holder retires, which-ever comes later	None
Taxes at Death	100% taxed at income	Tax free provided All IRS requirements are met.	Tax Free

Five Reasons to Invest in After-Tax Accounts

In summary, here's why you should invest in a tax-advantaged after-tax account instead of a 401(k) plan.

You're taxed at the capital gains level. When the government established 401(k) plans in 1980, it ran projections showing that if you get a tax deduction at the time of investment, if the assets grow tax-deferred, and if you withdraw the money at a lower tax rate, you end up with more money. The government was right in those projections. However—and this is a huge however—the government changed the rules along the way. It lowered the capital gains tax rate. When 401(k) plans were established, income and capital gains were taxed at the same rate. Today and for the foreseeable future, federal income is taxed at a maximum of 37%, and capital gains are taxed at a maximum of 20%. So at the time of distribution and death, the money in your 401(k) plan will always be taxed at the higher income rate, and not at the lower capital gains rate.

It allows for a step-up in cost basis. To recap, a step-up in cost basis is a tax code provision that allows the cost of an appreciated asset, upon inheritance, to be adjusted for tax purposes. With a step-up in cost basis, the value of the asset is the market value of the asset at the time of inheritance, not the market value at which the asset was purchased—and the former is usually higher. The step-up in cost basis is the single biggest tax break the IRS gives us, and it does not apply to retirement accounts.

You get to choose exactly what you want to sell. You probably know what cost basis is: essentially, the original value of an investment (usually the purchase price). The difference between the cost basis of an investment and its current market value is your capital gain. Often, when selling an investment, investors will choose which "lot" to sell based on cost basis. For example, let's say you have 100 shares of stock. You purchased 50 shares at $50 a share, and 50 shares at $100 a share. Now, you want to sell 50 shares at the market price of $125 per share. Chances are you'd choose to sell the lot of shares you purchased at $100, because then your capital gain would be only $25 per share. But that matters only in an after-tax account. With a 401(k) plan, all before-tax contributions have a cost basis of zero. As a result, it doesn't matter which ones you withdraw, and every dollar withdrawn is taxed as income. You lose an important means of managing your investments for tax efficiency.

You have total access to your money. Tax-managed accounts have none of the withdrawal restrictions 401(k) plans do. You can access any amount of money you want, at any time.

In conclusion, your long-term investments must navigate not only the markets but also the tax code—and as long as the tax code is structured so that income is taxed at a higher rate than capital gains, and there's a step-up in cost basis for after-tax accounts, your 401(k) plan will likely be the most taxed of all your assets. Now that you know better, don't invest in a 401(k) plan. In avoiding this tax trap, you'll be joining every member of Congress. They don't have 401(k) plans, either. Maybe that should tell you something.

You aren't subject to required minimum distributions (RMDs). An RMD is, in many ways, the WMD (weapon of mass destruction) of retirement planning. It is a minimum amount of money you must withdraw annually from your retirement account, typically starting in the year that you reach seventy and a half years of age. RMDs apply to all employer-sponsored retirement plans, including profit-sharing plans, 401(k) plans, 403(b) plans, and 457(b) plans, as well as to traditional IRAs and IRA-based plans such as SEPs and SIMPLE IRAs. If you don't want to withdraw your money so it can keep growing, this could be a problem. That's another reason after-tax accounts may be preferable to many retirees. They don't have RMDs.

Closing

"The question isn't at what age I want to retire, it's at what income," said George Foreman, former pro boxer and entrepreneur.

Or, to quote an unknown sage, "Retirement: no job, no stress, no pay!"

Truer words have rarely been spoken (at least in terms of retirement planning), and they're particularly applicable to this conversation. How can you save and invest in a way that lets you reach your desired income level in retirement?

I approached that question in two ways in this book—negative and positive. So as I set you off to spread your wings and secure your own retirement, I'd like to leave you with two parting thoughts along those lines.

The Negative: Avoid 401(k) Plans

As I'm sure you've gathered by now, I'm not a fan of 401(k) plans. I hope I've helped you understand why, and shown you a better way to achieve a financially secure retirement.

But I don't want to be *too* negative. There's a lot to like about 401(k) plans, as I've explained.

- They allow you to save up to $18,000 a year, pretax, with an additional $6,000 catch-up contribution allowed for those age fifty and older.
- Many employers match part of your contribution, giving you what amounts to free money. This is the number-one reason you would want to invest in a 401(k) plan.

- You can direct the manner in which your 401(k) funds are invested, and you may have a lot of choices, depending on what your plan offers—stocks, bonds, cash, or a combination of stocks and bonds and cash, depending on the level of risk you can tolerate.
- Earnings derived from investments in a 401(k) plan are not taxed; they're reinvested, and compound over time.
- Finally, most 401(k) plans offer some level of flexibility if you're in a financial pinch. Depending on the circumstances, you can take a loan or a hardship withdrawal from your 401(k) plan. When you take a loan, you pay yourself back, meaning you collect the interest. That's better than a bank collecting the interest.

The problem, at its most basic level, comes down to taxes.

I showed you an example of two people—Mr. Uninformed and Mrs. Smart—who invested the same money in a 401(k) account and an after-tax account, and saw the money grow to the same amount at retirement.

Then Mr. Uninformed and Mrs. Smart retired and started a systematic withdrawal program, and that's where Mrs. Smart came out ahead, because she understood that not all taxes are the same. If you have to be taxed, you want to be taxed at the long-term capital-gains tax rate. Mr. Uninformed wasn't; Mrs. Smart was.

Mrs. Smart also benefitted upon her death. While her death was surely a tragedy to all who loved her, her children received a step-up in cost basis to the value of the account at the date of death—a provision that doesn't apply to retirement accounts such as Mr. Uninformed's.

Now, Mr. Uninformed did have one benefit Mrs. Smart didn't—employer matches, as I mentioned a few paragraphs ago. And that's why I said that if you receive a match, investing in a 401(k) plan isn't *quite* such a bad idea. But you should invest only up to the level of the company match. In other words, if your company matches up to 4%, contribute 4%—not a penny more.

I hope that makes sense, and you were able to digest the rest of the book with an eye toward other options—specifically, the steps I set out in my introduction. They're shown below.

I'm not going to rehash those steps; you already read them. But I am going to revisit what is arguably the second-most important point I made: how you can beat the rigged tax system that makes 401(k) plans too problematic.

"People feel like the system is rigged against them, and here is the painful part: they're right," said US Senator Elizabeth Warren. "The system is rigged."

*****

In Review

1: Pay off your debt.
2: Understand taxation.
3: Get the government out of your retirement plan.
4: Understand the evolution of the 401(k) plan.
5: Stop contributing to your 401(k) plan.
6: Don't assume you should put small-business profits in retirement plans.
7: Avoid target-date retirement funds.
8: Take these three steps to a secure low-tax retirement.

*****

The Positive: Save Your Age Divided by Three

I think there's a much better way to save for retirement than 401(k) plans—after tax accounts, with a bit of discipline thrown in.

Of course, discipline is the hard part. Few of us want to make our beds, go to the gym, and load the dishwasher. Those things aren't fun. It's the same with saving for retirement.

But, we desperately need to save for retirement. A stunning 21% of Americans have nothing at all saved for the future, and another

10% have less than $5,000 tucked away, according to Northwestern Mutual's 2018 Planning & Progress Study.

"You know that retirement is coming," said Batya Shevich in *Warren Buffett: To Be Rich And Successful Is Easy!* "It isn't as though it just shows up one day and takes you by surprise, so you need to get ready for it."

So how do you find the discipline to save? I introduced my secret sauce for that discipline: take your age, divide it by three, and save that percentage of your gross salary.

Granted, this process ends up being a bit more complex than it sounds—at least if you don't start early. So let me explain it again, in a slightly different way.

Say you're twenty-five, and earn $50,000 a year. Your age (twenty-five) divided by three is 8.33%, and 8.33% of $50,000 is $4,165. So you'll need to save $4,165 per year to get on the path to secure retirement. That's just $347 per month. That's not bad, right?

Now let's say you wait to age thirty-five to start saving, and you (unfortunately) still earn $50,000 a year. We take your age (thirty-five) and divide it by three for 11.67%. Then we add that 11.67% to the original 8.33% (your penalty for not saving sooner) for a total savings rate of 20%. So starting at age thirty-five, you will need to save 20% of your $50,000 salary—$10,000 a year, $833 a month. Ouch! You may need to give up vacations, dining out, and cars that run reliably.

Now consider what would happen if you wait until age forty-five to start saving, and still earn $50,000 a year. (Clearly, you should be looking for a job that offers annual inflation-or performance-based increases, but we'll ignore than for the purposes of this example.) Now you have to save your age (forty-five) divided by three, so 15%. And you would have to add to that 15% the 8.33% penalty for not starting to save at age twenty-five and the 11.67% penalty for not starting to save at age thirty-five, for a total savings rate of 35%. That would be $17,500 a year, or $1,458 a month. You'll barely be able to pay your bills. In fact, you'll probably have to move in with your parents, or worse, your children.

It may sound tough, but remember what Dave Ramsey, the personal finance guru, once said, "Live like no one else so later you can live and give like no one else."

All for You

To close, there's one final point I'd like to reiterate: none of this should discourage you from saving because you're convinced that you can't easily reach your goals.

Anything you can save today will make your life at least a little better tomorrow. And a little better counts for a lot.

I've advised many clients about money management over the years, and in the process, I've investigated every possible way to help people reach their retirement goals. And the first step to success has always been awareness. "Risk comes from not knowing what you're doing," said investing guru Warren Buffett.

If you don't prepare, you'll end up in the same boat as many Americans, toiling away your golden years. According to the National Institute on Retirement Security, the gap between what Americans have saved and what they will need in retirement is estimated to be between $6.8 and $14 trillion. It's no surprise, then, that many are choosing to work—at Walmart, Target, McDonalds, or other such establishments.

I hope, that with the help of this book, that won't be you.

So, here are the 3 takeaways from this book:

1. **Standard deduction:**
   The IRS does not tax the first $12,000 of earned income per person per year. Invest this into a tax-managed portfolio of no-load mutual funds that are suitable for your needs.

2. **Capital Gains deduction:**
   The IRS does not tax the first $38,600 of long term capital gains realized per person per year. You can withdraw

this amount annually Tax Free. Can be combined with #1 (standard deduction) bringing the annual tax free total to $50,600!

3. **Step up in basis:**
The IRS does not tax the first $11.4 million of assets passed to heirs. This can be used during life or at death. Pass your estate onto your loved ones Tax-Free.

Remember that old slogan "Nothing is certain except death and taxes". Now, it is just death.

Your Action plan:

1. Stop contributing to your 401(k) today and invest in an after tax account.
2. Pay down your debt as quickly as possible.
3. Save your age divided by three.

By doing this you will get off the 401(k) treadmill to nowhere and finally feel the wind in your face as you cruise down the 1099(m) highway to East Street. The first thing you are going to realize is that you don't see any of your family and friends on Easy Street. That doesn't mean you won't recognize anybody. You will see all the rich and famous people. Hey, wait a minute is that Warren Buffet and Jeff Bezos? Wow,

I really did make it! Congratulations!!

About the Author

Mark Anthony Grimaldi is a certified fund specialist, chief economist, and money manager for the Sector Rotation Fund (NAVFX), a noted economic forecaster, and an author. He is known for his accurate economic forecasts and sector-rotation method of money management.

Early Career

Grimaldi began his career in money management in 1986 as an investment coordinator at Meyer Handleman Company in New York. He worked as director of operations for as Prime Financial Services and manager of securities operations for Marshall & Sterling Consultants, and coordinated and taught securities training classes at Duchess Community College in Poughkeepsie, New York, from 1989 to 2005.

Portfolio Management

In 2008, Grimaldi became comanager for the Stadion Tactical Growth Fund (ETFOX). During his thirteen-month tenure, when he applied his sector rotation method, the fund's Morningstar rating increased from 1 star to 5 stars, and its assets under management increased almost 400%.

In December 2009, Grimaldi became chief economist and money manager of the NAVFX. In this role, Grimaldi used his thirty years of macroeconomic and investment-management experience to select the market sectors he believes have the most growth potential. As of April 30, 2019, NAVFX has a 5 star Morningstar Rating for the prior 3 and 5 years. More recent performance can be obtained from

Morningstar.com. The auhor doesn't guarantee the accuracy of any ranking services and knowledges that ranking can change at any time.

Economic Forecasting

During his career, Grimaldi forecasted a number of key economic events, including the following:

The 2007 housing-market correction. In March 2006, shortly before the S&P / Case-Shiller Home Price Index reached an all-time high of 188.93, Grimaldi wrote in his Navigator newsletter, "In the next five years, house values are going to return to their 1997 levels plus inflation." In the second quarter of 2009, the S&P / Case-Shiller Home Price Index reached a low of 111.11.

The 2008 gold-market rally. In January 2007, when gold was selling at $625 per ounce, Grimaldi wrote in his Navigator newsletter, "My long-shot prediction of the year is gold (the single worst asset class over the last 10 years) will rally." In his January 2008 newsletter, Grimaldi continued this thought, writing that gold would reach $1,000 per ounce, and in his January 2009 newsletter, he changed his prediction to $1,100 per ounce. In May 2008 gold reached $1,000 per ounce, and in November 2009 it reached $1,100 per ounce.

The 2008–2009 recession. In his December 2007 Navigator newsletter, Grimaldi wrote that "recession risk increased from 60 percent to 70 percent in 2008," and in his January 2008 newsletter, he wrote that "a recession begins in the middle of the year." Looking back, we now know that a recession formally began in December 2007, and lasted eighteen months, until June 2009.

Skyrocketing unemployment. In January 2009, when the national unemployment rate was under 7%, Grimaldi wrote in his Navigator newsletter that unemployment would reach 10% nationally. On November 6, 2009, it did.

The 2010 "flash crash." In his January 2010 Navigator newsletter, Grimaldi called for "the first 1,000-point down day in the history of the Dow Jones Industrial Average in 2010." In the flash crash—the quick drop in stock prices that occurred on May 6, 2010—the Dow plunged approximately 1,000 points.

The Money Compass

In 2014 Grimaldi coauthored *The Money Compass*, a plain-English guide to good investing that presents practical strategies and actionable advice for safely navigating today's financial markets (Wiley). From the book's description:

> Between the ongoing recession, the collapse of the housing market, and the crumbling of the middle class, many Americans are left wondering what happened to the American Dream. They're also wondering what happened to their money. For millions of people, just making ends meet is challenging enough. So, when it comes to saving and investing, it seems like the deck is stacked against you.
>
> The bad news is that you're right. If the economy were a card game, the dealer would hold all the aces. But the good news is that you don't have to play by the house rules. Renowned for his unvarnished insight on finance and investing, money manager Mark Grimaldi has a reputation for telling it like it is. He doesn't sugarcoat the negative and he doesn't have time for the financial industry hype that leads to bad investing decisions. Here's the truth: the economy is in bad shape, but that doesn't mean you can't save responsibly, invest profitably, and retire comfortably.
>
> In *The Money Compass*, Grimaldi teams up with accounting professor G. Stevenson Smith to offer a wealth of smart investing advice for today's investor. This plain-English guide to good investing presents practical strategies and actionable advice for safely navigating today's financial markets. It shows you how to manage credit and debt responsibly, how to use the tax code to

> your advantage, which kinds of trendy investing advice you should ignore, and where to put your money for solid returns.
>
> In addition, the authors explore the hard-macroeconomic realities that explain how we got here and where we're going next. They look at the primary causes and consequences of the recession, the housing crash, the slow collapse of government programs, long-term unemployment, and how it all impacts you and your money. Plus, Grimaldi and Stevenson forecast the next big economic shock and show you how to profit from it.
>
> The economic game is rigged to keep you poor and keep Wall Street rich. So, it's time to write your own rules. Whether your white collar, blue collar, or somewhere in between, *The Money Compass* gives you the commonsense guidance you need to chart a course to a comfortable financial future—even in the roughest economic waters.

Reviews of *The Money Compass* have been overwhelmingly positive.

> I, like many Americans, have found myself sitting in the wasteland that once was my financial life. It seems nearly impossible to get ahead in these times. What am I doing wrong? How can I change this? These and many other questions I asked myself over the past 5 or 6 years. And then comes *The Money Compass*. Wow! Never have I read such a clear and concise synopsis on the economic world at large. Chapter after chapter provided not only new insights, but confirmations of my past actions… Sure, I made poor choices,

but then, so did most folks. Rather than berating, the authors help us to understand how we ALL got here, who did it to us, and even give thoughts on how to avoid the same messes again. Thanks, these words of wisdom, I feel better prepared to watch my financial back, protect what I have, and make better choices to get ahead in the future. Well written and an easy read, I'd recommend this to anyone who needs to regain their financial "bearing."

Probably the one thing that most people worry about is money. It seems you can never have too much but always there is too little. In *The Money Compass* by Mark Grimaldi and Stevenson Smith you are given tools that help you take a proactive role in your own wealth.

This book is more than a preachy account of what you need to do, it is actually a good teacher in what you should do. There are many insightful exercises and tips on things you should do that you probably did not think about.

The US has is slowly inching itself out of the great recession of 2008 and regardless of your situation you should not be caught in the next one (which the author predicts is around the corner).

Money is only paper and you need to take charge and steer the financial waters with a steady hand and the helpful book *The Money Compass.*

The Money Compass By Mark Grimaldi is an intellectual feast: referring back to the "America that once was." Mr. Grimaldi (the writer of the former "Money Navigator Newsletter," now the "Money Compass" newsletter), has a knack for explaining finance in a down to earth, easy to understand manner. I read the entire book in two sittings and urged my wife to read it as well. Mark is a conservative economist, so he explains the economy based on Wall St. and Washington. He discusses the "pickle" our country is in, from the "Federal Debt Bomb" to student loans to the lobbyists in DC. The subtitle: "Where Your Money Went and How to Get It Back" is an apt synopsis.

I am terribly afraid that America is on its way to becoming a "third world" country: Mr. Grimaldi with advice like "Live Below Your Means" and acquire "Academic Skills" is right on target. How in the world will we pay off 17 TRILLION $ of debt??

I would suggest you buy this book and keep a notepad nearby: you will surely benefit. Near the end, there are quotes of the economic forecasts the newsletter has made over the years. He predicts a 2014 recession…Hold on to your hat! (and your money): get this extraordinary book that is a "Compass" to guide you through the world of finance.

Mark Grimaldi's *The Money Compass* points readers to sound waters. It begins with perspective on the erosion of national fiscal sanity and its consequences for both the society and the individual. It makes a clear case that traditional devices for preserving wealth have gone by the wayside in recent decades. While much of the survival advice is modest and workable for the average person, quite a bit is very high-powered, and makes the case for engaging a financial advisor. The lesson is clear: having a compass in hand is useful, but it takes more than one hand to steer your vessel into safe harbors.

Education

Grimaldi received a bachelor's degree in economics from Albany State University in 1985. He holds the Certified Fund Specialist (CFS) designation.

CPSIA information can be obtained
at www.ICGtesting.com
Printed in the USA
JSHW020507230920
8164JS00002B/4